CHECK

Practical Checklists for Leaders

THIRD EDITION

JAY R. DESKO, PH.D.,
DAVID A. MARKS, D.MIN.

Acknowledgments

The Center Consulting Group is a Christian organization with a highly trained team that is passionate about advancing leadership and organizational health. We believe this resource on practical actions for leaders will be helpful for you and your organization. We are providing this resource as an extension of our vision of advancing organizational health.

© 2022, 2013, 2011 by Jay R. Desko and David A. Marks. All rights reserved. Distributed by The Center Consulting Group. Reprinted with permission.

ISBN: 978-1-7923-9771-4

Third edition published October 2022.

Layout & design by Tiehl McRoberts.

Cover art & design by Sarah Derstein.

While The Center Consulting Group and the authors have used their best efforts in producing this book, they make no representations with respect to the accuracy or completeness of its contents. The advice provided may not be appropriate for your specific organizational situation. You should seek professional counsel where appropriate.

*All characters appearing in this work are fictitious. Any resemblance to real persons, living or dead, is purely coincidental.

For more information about The Center Consulting Group, visit our website at www.centerconsulting.org or call 215-723-2325.

Contents

1. Communication

2. Character & Credibility

3. Motivation & Influence

4. Critical Thinking

5. Emotional & Relational Growth

6. Change & Momentum

7. Teamwork & Supervision

8. Personal Growth & Development

9. Planning & Organizing

10. Leadership

Introduction

What do flying a plane and leading an organization have in common? They both need a plan! While there are many books and resources on planning, what is often needed is a simple checklist to ensure the most important things are not forgotten. It is for this reason that a pilot conducts a preflight check before every departure. No need to remember and recall all the details and run the risk of forgetting something important – just check the list! This book is, by design, rather simple. It is a book of checklists for each of the areas important to any leader.

The art of communication is the
language of leadership.

JAMES HUMES

CHAPTER ONE

Communication

✅ 4 Types of Communicators

Passive

Passive communicators do not share their personal concerns readily. They defer to others, especially to those in charge or who have a dominating presence. They speak low and slow, and they appear to lack confidence or competency. They are often not trusted because others do not know what they are really thinking.

Aggressive

Aggressive communicators are quick to share their opinion or preferences with little regard for others or the context. They are poor listeners but will engage verbally with those that disagree. They frequently interrupt and get louder and more dogmatic if met with resistance. They will use intimidation, sarcasm, humiliation, or endless questioning to gain the upper hand. Their body language will indicate irritation with anyone who disagrees.

Passive and Aggressive

Like a snake in the grass, passive and aggressive communicators appear harmless but then strike without notice. Their body language does not match how they actually feel. Appearing to be cooperative, they subtly and purposely do things to sabotage a person or process. This style is most commonly manifested in people who are resentful or feel powerless.

Assertive

Assertive communicators can stay focused on the mission because they "say what they mean, and mean what they say." Others know where those who are assertive stand because they respectfully and clearly advocate for their own needs without violating the rights of others. They value themselves, their time, and their physical and emotional needs.

10 Skills for Effective Facilitation

1. Preparing for the meeting.
2. Observing group dynamics.
3. Asking questions.
4. Listening attentively.
5. Encouraging others.
6. Summarizing discussion.
7. Giving feedback.
8. Defining problems.
9. Guiding discussion.
10. Confronting unhealthy behavior.

7 Common Facilitation Mistakes

1. Failing to define the group's purpose and expectations.
2. Allowing a few people to dominate.
3. Refusing to address unhealthy behaviors.
4. Allowing the group to drift far from the task.
5. Talking too much.
6. Failing to encourage all members to participate.
7. Managing the group's time poorly.

✅ The Communication Process

MESSAGE

What is the focused message I am intending to send?

CHANNEL

What is the BEST way to send the message to my audience?

FILTERS

What will likely help or hinder my message from being heard as intended?

RECEIVER

How did the receiver respond or react to your intended message?

FEEDBACK

Does the feedback require I alter or clarify my intended message?

Best Practices of World-Class Speakers

1. Know your topic and your audience well.
2. Dress appropriately for the occasion.
3. Start your talk with a thought-provoking illustration, question, or story.
4. Use relevant humor and stories.
5. Use appropriate body language.
6. Maintain eye contact with your audience.
7. Avoid being monotone by using a variety of vocal inflections.
8. Be conscious of time; know when to stop talking.
9. Quote from others for confirmation or contrast.
10. Use technology only to supplement. Do not let it become a distraction.
11. If using technology, be sure to test it in advance.
12. Speak with confidence seasoned with humility.
13. Practice your delivery in advance, but strive to be yourself.
14. When finished, seek constructive feedback from a few trusted people.

✅ Quotable Quotes About Public Speaking

- "A wise man speaks because he has something to say, a fool speaks because he has to say something." – Plato

- "Remember not only to say the right thing in the right place, but far more difficult still, to leave unsaid the wrong thing at the tempting moment."
  – Benjamin Franklin

- "Be sincere; be brief; be seated." – Franklin D. Roosevelt

- "I've learned that people will forget what you said, people will forget what you did, but people will never forget how you made them feel." – Maya Angelou

- "It usually takes me more than three weeks to prepare a good impromptu speech." – Mark Twain

- "Speech is power: speech is to persuade, to convert, to compel." – Ralph Waldo Emerson

- "Only a fool says everything that is on his mind."
  – Proverbs 29:11

- "A wise man holds his tongue. Only a fool blurts out everything he knows." – Proverbs 10:14

Public Speaking Evaluation Chart

Use this chart to identify the areas of your greatest strengths and weaknesses as a public speaker. Place a plus (+) next to your top five strengths and a minus (-) next to your top perceived weaknesses. Use the evaluation of your public speaking proficiency to maximize your strengths when preparing your delivery and also to develop a plan to mitigate the areas where you lack confidence or skills. Seeking feedback from others using this list can be humbling but helpful.

- [ ] Freedom from notes
- [ ] Absence of bias
- [ ] Intentional eye contact with participants
- [ ] Coordinated use of gestures
- [ ] Warmth/connection with the audience
- [ ] Clarity of the BIG idea
- [ ] Relevant illustrations
- [ ] Practical application
- [ ] Use of story
- [ ] Insert pithy, thought-provoking quotes
- [ ] Appropriate humor
- [ ] Effective use of technology

- [ ] Meaningful data/facts
- [ ] Balance of humility and confidence
- [ ] Convincing/compelling
- [ ] Inspirational
- [ ] Believability/credibility
- [ ] Reasonable/logical
- [ ] Time management
- [ ] Diction/pronunciation
- [ ] Avoid filler words (um, ah)
- [ ] Grammar/vocabulary
- [ ] Pace (speed of speaking)
- [ ] Pitch (voice variation)

The 6 C's of Communication

Use this list to prepare communication such as emails, reports, presentations, and personal conversations.

1. Credible

Do you have the responsibility and authority to be sending this message? When your message is received, it should add credence to the values of your organization. Is your communication authentic, accurate, and aimed at the right audience? Consistently credible communication will strengthen trust and provide stability during difficult situations.

2. Clarity

Lack of clarity leads to misaligned expectations. Every message should have a (singular) specific and clearly stated goal for the particular audience that is receiving the communication. The chief purpose/desired outcome of the communication should be able to be stated in one sentence. When practical, send separate communications if there are multiple subjects or purposes to be achieved. After receiving the message, the recipient should know who, what, when, why, and whether action on their part is expected, optional, or required.

3. Concise

The shorter, the better! Skillful communication requires mastering the art of being concise. Practice eliminating filler words from your writing and speaking. Adjectives like "for instance," "you see," "definitely," "kind of," "literally," "basically," or "I mean" are unnecessary. Redundancy should be avoided.

4. Courtesy

Seek to set a positive, friendly, open, and honest tone. Avoid comments that could be viewed as insulting, insensitive, or passive-aggressive. Sarcasm can often be misinterpreted in written communications. Begin with the assumption that your communication will be widely distributed even if you are writing to just one person. Courtesy is a way to show respect and earn respect.

5. Correct

Error-free communication adds to your credibility. Conversely, you lose credibility and show unintended disrespect to your recipients when your communication contains errors. Check dates, times, places, names, and titles mentioned in your message. It is wise to have someone proofread the text of your communication for grammatical errors, spelling, phraseology, and use of technical terms if your communication is going to be widely distributed or used in an official capacity.

6. Coherent

Written communication varies greatly from oral communication. Does your message flow smoothly and have a logical sequence? Avoid assuming that your recipients all share the same information. Based on the context, it may be appropriate to give a short executive summary of the critical elements needed to correctly understand the intention of your message. Additionally, depending on your audience, you may need to craft separate messages in order to be most coherent to that group.

10 Digital Communication Reminders

1. The Golden Rule
Treat others as you would like to be treated.

2. No "Trolling"
Trolling is a form of verbal abuse when you intentionally attack or disrespect someone online for whatever reason. Maybe you didn't agree with something they said, but there's a nice way to share a different point of view without name-calling or attacking someone. Avoid the read-and-reply tendency if you are irritated. Vent-and-send does not usually yield the results you intend. Do not confront via electronic communication. Send a non-defensive invitation to meet face-to-face.

3. DON'T TYPE IN ALL CAPS
It hurts our eyes. It makes people think you are shouting at them. It's okay to type in caps to accentuate a word or two, but please don't do it all the time everywhere you go. Don't use the color red either.

4. Don't Spam
Be careful that you don't inadvertently pass along the names and email addresses of others. Use the "Bcc" block (blind copy) when sending a message to a group.

5. Limit the Lingo
Emailing, messaging, texting, blogging, etc. have all become quite informal. The use of initials, codes, jargon, and emojis can be fun and efficient but can be easily overdone. Especially in professional communications, limit the trendy, casual, and often mysterious lingo.

6. To Quote or Not to Quote

Just because information is on the internet or comes from a trusted friend does not make it correct. You will save yourself from great embarrassment by checking the accuracy of any data, stories, pictures, etc. Some of the sites dedicated to fact-checking have even proven vulnerable to misinformation.

7. Use Proper Grammar & Spelling

Use a platform that has a built-in spell check or type the message into a word processor (Microsoft Word, Notes, etc.) and then paste it into your email or text. Typos and spelling mistakes will happen, but they can distract from your message.

8. Keep It "G" Rated

As a general rule, don't write or say anything you wouldn't let your kids read. If you forward something inappropriate because you find it funny, you can be certain someone else will find it funny and pass it along with your name attached. Additionally, digital conversation is "flat" and can be easily misunderstood. Because of the absence of facial cues, messages can be interpreted as criticism or antagonism. Discretion is needed.

9. Maintain Privacy

Comments made during electronic discussions are generally considered confidential. However, do not assume what you communicate will be held in confidence – assume it will be passed on. If you are concerned about this, specifically request your recipient to not forward your communication.

10. Avoid Inflammatory Language

Above all, avoid inflammatory language and topics that are not suited to be resolved or addressed over social media.

Perceptual Positioning

The best communicators have developed the skill to perceptually reposition themselves to see a situation from multiple viewpoints. This results in better critical thinking, problem-solving, and resolution. In conflict resolution, a moderator can assist the conflicting parties to walk through the perceptual positioning process until they come to an amicable and wise agreement.

To walk the bases of perceptual positioning, put four pieces of paper on the ground and physically move from position to position. At each position, ask, "What are the needs, wants, concerns, and pressures this person is facing?"

Position #1: Your View/Self

Think of your perspective and opinion. Articulate accurately how you see a situation. Provide rationale for your opinion that is NOT emotionally charged or skewed by personal bias.

Position #2: Their View/Other

Think of the other person's perspective and opinion. Put yourself in the "other guy's shoes." Without sarcasm, honestly try and express the logic, motive, and goals of those who oppose or disagree with you.

Position #3: Observer View

Step outside of the situation. Like a jury, objectively weigh the merits of each of the positions and make a decision about what seems like the best/wisest scenario or conclusion for the organization.

Position #4: Stakeholder View

Did the leaders act maturely and in my best interest or did their egos get in the way of making a good decision?

PERCEPTUAL POSITIONING

#2
THEIR VIEW
(OTHER)

#3
OBSERVER
VIEW

What are the needs, wants, concerns, and pressures of each viewpoint?

#1
YOUR VIEW
(SELF)

#4
STAKEHOLDER
VIEW

✅ Communicating with Candor

Our goals as leaders, managers, and friends should be to communicate with compassionate candor – speaking to others in a way that is both forthright AND caring; this can also be referred to as "constructive engagement." Remember that not everything we see in someone needs to be addressed. But behaviors or shortcomings that can cause harm to ourselves, to our organizations, or to others need constructive engagement.

Why is compassionate candor/constructive engagement not more common? The primary answer is FEAR. Fear of losing a relationship, losing a job or opportunity for advancement, and fear of the stress and awkwardness that come with being forthright. Remember this: when considering candor, people

CARING	SHORTSIGHTED SYMPATHY	CONSTRUCTIVE ENGAGEMENT
	Common labels: Caring. Withholding. Fearful.	Common labels: Genuine. Courageous. Fair.
	Consider: Speak truth to one another. Eph. 4:25	Consider: Treat others as you wish to be treated. Luke 6:31
	PASSIVE INSTIGATION	DESTRUCTIVE AGGRESSION
	Common labels: Political. Manipulative. Triangulation.	Common labels: Arrogant. Provoking. Damaging.
	Consider: Don't grumble among one another. John 6:43	Consider: Clothe yourself in humility. 1 Peter 5:5

CONFRONTING

tend to overestimate the potential for bad outcomes and underestimate the potential for good outcomes.

How to Move Towards Compassionate Candor

If you are on the giving end of compassionate candor:

1. Know yourself: Which quadrant am I normally in and why?

2. Ask yourself: What is the issue, and is it important enough or necessary?

3. Prepare yourself: Balance care and confrontation by being…

   Direct: Talk directly to the person rather than talking to everyone else about him or her.

   Specific: Give examples or illustrations that would help the person better understand what you are talking about and why it is important.

   Non-punishing: Use language and tone that are adequate for the person to hear you in light of his or her unique personality, but do not be damaging or toxic. As a general rule, if you are angry, wait.

And if you are on the receiving end of compassionate candor:

1. Defensiveness is normal, so be aware and manage it.

2. Be humble enough to listen respectfully.

3. Seek feedback BEFORE it comes to you unsolicited.

Nonverbal Communicators

The use of technology has an upside and a downside. Social media, email, cell phones, and a myriad of other means of communication have increased the volume of communication, but they may have lowered the overall quality of communication that can only be achieved through face-to-face conversations. Younger generations tend to "text" rather than "talk" to their friends when they are not together.

Most experts agree that the majority of the message (up to 70%) is transmitted not by words but through means of nonverbal signaling, even during person-to-person communication. Nonverbal cues enhance our understanding of what is really being said when people talk. Here are examples of nonverbal communicators.

1. **Facial expressions** (smile, frown, tight lips)
2. **Gestures** (pointing, waving, gesturing)
3. **Paralinguistics** (pitch, pace, volume, laughing, crying, yawning, sighing)
4. **Closeness** (proximity, distance apart, obstructed view via walls, cubicles)
5. **Eye contact and movements** (squinting, blinking, staring, winking, rolling)
6. **Haptics/feelings via touch** (handshake, hugging, kissing, back slap, "high-five," shoulder pat)
7. **Appearance** (posture, unkempt, formal, casual, messy, tidy)

8. **Artifacts/symbols** (credentials, labels, jewelry, tattoos, piercings, decorations, furnishings)

9. **Body language** (slouching, arms crossed, nodding, head down, doodling, checking phone)

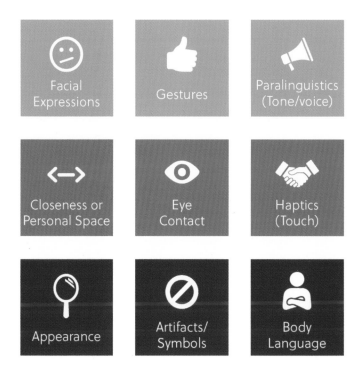

The single biggest problem in communication is the illusion that it has taken place.

– *George Bernard Shaw*

Reputation is for a time; character is for eternity.

J. B. GOUGH

CHAPTER TWO

Character & Credibility

4 Discernment Deterrents

1. Pride

Pride, an inordinately high opinion of one's dignity, importance, merit, or superiority, is perhaps the most powerful deterrent to discernment. The Bible is full of examples of God accusing both nations and people of pride and warning that He hates it (Proverbs 8:13) and that the proud man or nation will ultimately fall (Proverbs 16:18). In one study, pride and narcissism were identified as two of the top reasons why intelligent people make dumb choices[1]. Self-centeredness, entitlement, an inflated view of self, and a sense of invulnerability – all traits that can result in overconfidence – frequently characterize narcissistic leaders. All of these traits often lead to not seeking or listening to counsel, overvaluing one's own opinion, minimizing situations, and overestimating any ability to handle the challenge.

2. Self-Justification/Rationalization

A second contributing factor to failed discernment is self-justification or rationalization. When a leader demonstrates errors in judgment, he might own those errors at first, but his ownership is often temporary. In fact, it is quite common to see leaders shift from taking responsibility to justifying their mistakes. Why? Psychologists refer to the underlying cause as "cognitive dissonance." People cannot hold two inconsistent or conflicting beliefs in their minds for an extended period (such as *I made a serious mistake* and *I am an extraordinary leader*). As a result, the leader must justify why he is more correct and why others are less correct. This need to justify is why leaders are likely to align with people whose ideas agree

---

1   Mortimer Feinberg and John Tarrant, *Why Smart People Do Dumb Things*, 1995.

with their own, and why they either distance themselves from or seek to discredit the ideas of those who differ. And once a leader makes up his mind, he develops an army of reinforcing reasons to justify why he is correct, making it hard for anyone or anything to alter his thinking. By then, changing his mind holds too much risk.

3. Spiritualization

A third contributing factor to failed discernment is "spiritualization." Spiritualization can take many forms, including "playing the God card" or claiming an epiphany relating to the discernment process. This approach simplifies challenges and seldom leads to wise decisions. Some likely causes for this are:

1. When we want something very badly.

2. When we feel overwhelmed, pressured, or fatigued.

3. When we are proud or overconfident.

4. When we circle ourselves with those who think similarly.

5. When we discount, dismiss, or discredit opposing opinions.

4. Poor Relational and Emotional Management

A fourth contributing factor to failed discernment is poor relational and emotional management. Some of the most common leadership blind spots we see are when leaders do not know how to understand and manage their own emotions or how to adequately connect to those around them. People who have authentic relationships and understand unspoken relational cues that others send are more likely to use those cues in managing their behaviors and in seeking feedback from those around them formally and informally. Executive coach Marshall Goldsmith notes that the higher a person rises in position, the more pronounced their relational strengths or shortcomings are, and the greatest tool to help them is feedback[2].

Examples we have seen of poor relational management include:

- Failing to see the deterioration of their relational power.
- Verbally exploding when triggered the wrong way.
- Withholding their feelings about someone or something.
- Having difficulty showing empathy to others.
- Failing to see the frustration they are causing in others.
- Lacking accurate awareness of themselves including skills and behaviors.
- Failing to adequately communicate their expectations and ideas.
- Inadequately listening to what others are saying.
- Not spending regular time connecting with others.
- Having trouble connecting with others emotionally.
- Appearing awkward in normal social conversation and settings.
- Inflexible and unwilling to ever compromise or give in to others.
- Reframing the facts to fit the desired narrative.

---

2   Marshall Goldsmith, *What Got You Here Won't Get You There*, 2007.

In his book *Primal Leadership*, Daniel Goleman describes the emotional nature of two types of leaders: **resonant leaders** and **dissonant leaders**. The resonant leader manifests behaviors that attract others resulting in relational connection, happiness, and a positive environment. Dissonant leaders manifest behaviors that push others away resulting in conflict, fear, avoidance, and a negative environment.

12 Defensive Routines of Leaders

When leaders allow fear, pride, or threats to drive their behavior, they will respond with defensive routines which contribute to a culture of dysfunction. Here are 12 defensive routines of leaders.

1. Blaming others.
2. Justifying your choices.
3. Avoiding those who disagree.
4. Denying the facts.
5. Withholding information.
6. Intimidating through anger.
7. Deflecting others away from the topic.
8. Running away or quitting.
9. Spiritualizing your choices.
10. Recruiting supporters to your side.
11. Vilifying those who disagree.
12. Manipulating by way of fake humility.

16 Warning Signs of Abuse of Power

1. Assumes his/her vision is correct.

2. Assumes others are visionless.

3. Promotes unrealistic ideas.

4. Acquires dangerous power.

5. Blames others for failure.

6. Creates unhealthy dependence.

7. Discourages questioning.

8. Associates only with those who agree.

9. Convinces others their vision is righteous.

10. Withholds information to accomplish their goals.

11. Focuses on short-term success.

12. More likely to burn out quickly.

13. Refrains from building authentic relationships.

14. Depends upon rhetorical skills to cover problems.

15. Expects others to be like them.

16. Transfers focus to themselves.

> Nearly all men can stand adversity, but if you want to test a man's character, give him power.
>
> – *Robert Ingersoll about Abraham Lincoln*

✅ 12 Signs of Distrust

1. Excessive reliance on policies.
2. Fear of challenging authority.
3. Avoidance of difficult subjects.
4. Increased cliques.
5. Decreased social interaction.
6. Reduced enjoyment.
7. Second-guessing most decisions.
8. Increase of critical discussions behind closed doors.
9. Heavy dependence on hierarchal structures.
10. Atmosphere of suspicion and tension.
11. Intentionally withholding information.
12. Significant turnover of employees and constituents.

✅ 7 Traits of Trusting Teams

1. Taking responsibility for your actions.
2. Seeking input and advice.
3. Creating a safe environment for asking questions.
4. Believing the best in others until otherwise proven.
5. Regularly providing encouragement and affirmation.
6. Resolving conflicts quickly.
7. Pursuing relationships with others on the team.

6 Trust Filters

People trust you to meet their expectations of you. Even if their expectations are faulty, they are constantly filtering, consciously or unconsciously, their experiences with you in the following six areas. If you meet their expectations of you in these areas, your credibility will increase. If you fail to meet their expectations, your credibility will decrease.

1. **Character:** Speaking truthfully and acting with integrity.

2. **Concern:** Showing genuine love for and interest in others.

3. **Communication:** Sharing information regularly with others so they succeed.

4. **Competence:** Demonstrating growing skills in what you do.

5. **Connectedness:** Spending time with others giving and receiving grace (help).

6. **Courage:** Standing up for what is right and best for the cause.

> Character cannot be developed in ease and quiet. Only through experiences of trial and suffering can the soul be strengthened, vision cleared, ambition inspired, and success achieved.
>
> – Helen Keller

How Credibility Works

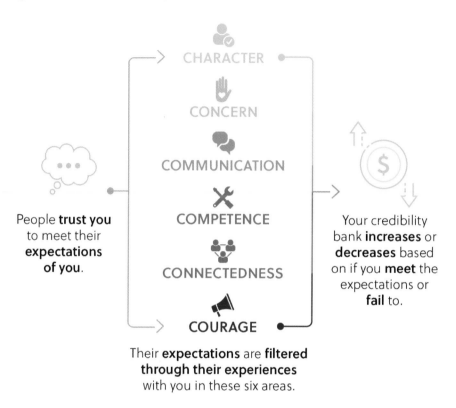

CHARACTER

CONCERN

COMMUNICATION

COMPETENCE

CONNECTEDNESS

COURAGE

People **trust you** to meet their **expectations of you**.

Your credibility bank **increases** or **decreases** based on if you **meet** the expectations or **fail** to.

Their **expectations** are **filtered through their experiences** with you in these six areas.

Credibility coins are given to those who have earned the trust of others by consistently meeting the expectations of those they serve.

A "full" **credibility bank** gives the owner enormous influence to lead change, develop other leaders, and take risks to get greater rewards.

Credibility coins are hard to get but easy to lose!

✅ 8 Things to Know About Credibility

1. Everyone has expectations (trust filters) of others required before "giving them credibility."

2. Credibility is essential to leadership and influence.

3. Our credibility "bank" is continually active.

4. We do not have complete control over our credibility bank.

5. Withdrawals for unfavorable behavior are often greater in magnitude than the deposits for favorable behavior.

6. The bank can be too inflated – reducing accountability.

7. The bank can be overdrawn – resulting in bankruptcy.

8. Some things are worth the loss of our credibility.

✅ The Cycle of Leadership Erosion

Declining Relationship and Trust

Expectations

RESULTS:
Loss of relationship
Loss of trust
Disillusionment and stress
Decreased effectiveness

Disappointment, Anger, Avoidance

Failure to Meet Expectations

CONTRIBUTING FACTORS INCLUDE:
Insufficient relational connection
Insufficient fit and chemistry
Inability to manage conflict effectively
Inadequate early intervention
Absence of a unifying vision
Lack of courage to act

15 Things That Will Deplete Your Credibility Bank

Credibility is very easy to lose but takes work to build and maintain. Why? Because credibility withdrawals for unfavorable behaviors are often greater in magnitude than the deposits for favorable behaviors. Here are 15 things that will quickly deplete your credibility bank and subsequently chip away at your leadership influence.

1. Having insufficient knowledge.

2. Limited input from others.

3. Ignorance.

4. Careless/inaccurate research.

5. Outdated data.

6. Manipulation of data.

7. Avoidance due to fear.

8. Arrogance/abuse of power.

9. Lack of follow-through and empty promises.

10. Hypocrisy/duplicity.

11. Lack of authenticity.

12. Minimization.

13. Exaggeration.

14. Confirmation bias/omission.

15. Dishonesty.

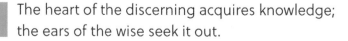

The heart of the discerning acquires knowledge; the ears of the wise seek it out.

– Psalm 18:15

✅ 11 Behaviors That Build Credibility

1. Always act with integrity.
2. Continually develop your gifts and sharpen your skills.
3. Do what you say you will do. Diligently follow through.
4. Empower and trust others and help them succeed.
5. Admit mistakes quickly and try to correct them.
6. Solve problems and help others do the same.
7. Recognize (publicly and privately) others' contributions.
8. Listen to suggestions and feedback.
9. Obtain endorsements from others with credibility.
10. Share information openly and freely.
11. Be accessible and visible.

✅ 5 Ways to Assess Your Credibility

1. Identify the people who are most important to the success of your leadership and attempt to assess how much credibility you have with them.
2. Seek feedback from other mature leaders regarding their perception of your credibility.
3. What behaviors, decisions, and actions have cost you the most credibility? Were they worth it?
4. What upcoming changes will require significant credibility? Do you have enough credibility to succeed in this change?
5. What should you start to do to improve your credibility?

8 Actions That Will Build Trust in an Epidemic of Distrust

1. Start with trust.

"I will never trust them again!" Those are the words of a person who has been hurt and disappointed. But, if we consistently start with distrust, it will result in distrust coming back to us. Distrust breeds distrust, and trust breeds trust. Even when someone has violated our trust, we must discerningly trust once again or they will never be able to rise above it.

2. Show genuine concern.

People trust those who genuinely care about them. Leaders often live emotionally distant from those around them. This results in lower trust.

3. Spend time together.

I once had a negative view of another leader. But when I had the opportunity to get to know him, we became good friends! By spending time with him, I got to know him more accurately. That is the benefit of spending time together.

4. Do what you say.

Politicians and most others who are trying to land a job have a propensity to make promises, some of which will be impossible to fulfill. Leaders promise to be "team-centered" and "collaborative" but sometimes fail to do so. If we want people to trust us, we would be wise to do what we say.

5. Tell the truth.

One lie can erase years of telling the truth. This is true in all relationships including work, marriage, and friendship. As a leader, I can tell the truth three hundred times, but if I fudge it or straight out lie once, the three hundred times of truthfulness will be forgotten, far overshadowed by the one lie.

6. Be transparent.

One of my clients is a master of this. He is quick to stand in front of others and acknowledge his mistakes, fears, and failures. And the result is that hundreds of people love working for him and many leaders seek him out for counsel. Transparency builds trust by showing others that you trust them with your less impressive aspects. People appreciate knowing you are like them – imperfect.

7. Be competent.

Competence is essential to forming trust, but it most often builds trust only when a certain skill set is needed. For example, when my daughter needed brain surgery as a child, we were not expecting to have the surgeon become our BFF. We just wanted the best surgeon we could find. He was a world-class neurosurgeon but with a personality that was a bit intimidating and cold. I had full confidence in him as a surgeon. And that was all I was looking for.

8. Be realistic.

No one manifests trustworthiness 100% of the time. All of us eventually disappoint, forget something important, make a major mistake, etc. Perhaps one of the challenges we face in declining trust is not just people acting in untrustworthy ways, it may also be that we have unrealistic expectations. Since we are broken, none of us will succeed if the expectation is perfection. As Ecclesiastes 7:20 accurately states, "Surely there is not a righteous man on earth who does good and never sins."

✅ Conducting a Trust Audit

Signs of Trust

- [ ] Regular time together as a team and with individuals.
- [ ] Problems are addressed quickly and constructively.
- [ ] Positive and enjoyable work environment.
- [ ] Freedom and encouragement to question authority.
- [ ] Mutual support for most significant decisions.
- [ ] Atmosphere of care and concern for one another.
- [ ] Information is freely shared between people/groups.
- [ ] Minimal suspicion regarding motives and decisions.
- [ ] Deepening level of dialogue over time.
- [ ] Delegation and minimal micro-management.
- [ ] Long-term retention of employees and constituents.
- [ ] Regular, unscheduled opportunities for dialogue.

Signs of Distrust

- [ ] Excessive reliance on policies.
- [ ] Fear of challenging authority.
- [ ] Avoidance of difficult subjects.
- [ ] Increased cliques.
- [ ] Decreased social interaction.
- [ ] Reduced enjoyment.
- [ ] Second-guessing most decisions.
- [ ] Increase of critical discussions behind closed doors.
- [ ] Heavy dependence on hierarchal structures.
- [ ] Atmosphere of suspicion and tension.
- [ ] Intentionally withholding information.
- [ ] Significant turnover of employees and constituents.

If your actions create a legacy that inspires others to dream more, learn more, do more and become more, then, you are an excellent leader.

DOLLY PARTON

CHAPTER THREE

Motivation & Influence

6 Ways to Develop Others

1. Believe others can lead as well as or better than yourself.

2. Train people not just to serve, but to lead.

3. Delegate real authority by treating others as leaders.

4. Coach others by providing assistance when they need it.

5. Encourage others to not grow weary in doing good.

6. Connect with others by spending relational time with them.

6 Questions to Improve the Performance of Others

1. Expectations: Do they know what is expected of them?

2. Feedback: Are you providing them with regular and clear feedback?

3. Resources: Do they have the resources to do what is expected of them?

4. Incentives: Are there incentives for exemplary performance?

5. Knowledge: Could they do the task if their lives depended upon it, and has appropriate training been provided?

6. Capacity: Do they have the physical, emotional, and spiritual capacity to do the task?

7 Ways to Build Your Leadership Influence

1. Never fudge the truth.
2. Do what you promise.
3. Admit your mistakes.
4. Solve problems quickly.
5. Show initiative.
6. Relate well to others.
7. Keep your skills sharpened.

7 Essential Transitions for a Growing Organization

1. Staff: From doers to developers.
2. Board: From micro oversight to macro.
3. Leadership: From good to great.
4. Members: From micro voice to macro.
5. Decisions: From centralized to decentralized.
6. Communication: From few mechanisms to many.
7. Trust: From important to essential.

> Sometimes when you innovate, you make mistakes. It is best to admit them quickly and get on with improving your other innovations.
>
> – *Steve Jobs*

✔ 5 Essential Transitions to Next Level Leadership

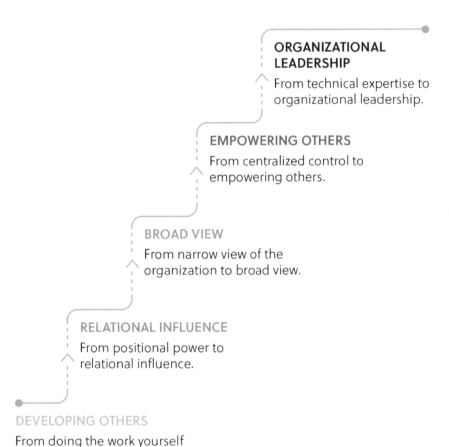

ORGANIZATIONAL LEADERSHIP
From technical expertise to organizational leadership.

EMPOWERING OTHERS
From centralized control to empowering others.

BROAD VIEW
From narrow view of the organization to broad view.

RELATIONAL INFLUENCE
From positional power to relational influence.

DEVELOPING OTHERS
From doing the work yourself to developing others.

7 Ways to Invest in a Younger Leader

We all had someone invest in us who influenced who we are today. Use these to invest in the younger leaders in your life!

1. Pick carefully
Select someone who you see high potential in, has a teachable attitude, and is a good fit with you.

2. Take risks
Allow the young leader to actually lead by entrusting them with valued opportunities.

3. Eat!
Spend time with the young leader beyond just work. Meals are a great starting place.

4. Share your credibility
Young leaders need you to loan some of your hard-earned credibility chips until they can earn their own.

5. Be natural
Don't try to make this robotic or programmatic. It's the relationship that counts the most!

6. Be transparent
Let them know not only about your successes but also about how you have failed and navigated those failures.

7. Learn from them
Young leaders not only have much to learn, but they also have much to share with us. Take advantage of their perspectives, knowledge, and experiences.

It takes approximately 10 years of hard work and the compilation of over one million patterns in order to develop expert intuition.

HERBERT SIMON

CHAPTER FOUR

Critical Thinking

✅ Understanding Critical Thinking

Critical thinking does not imply "negative" thinking, but rather it is a skill set that can assist the leader in discerning the "Next Right Step" for an individual or an organization. Critical thinking enables leaders to properly analyze, evaluate, problem-solve, and explain the rationale of their decisions to assure followers and stakeholders that they have acted with open-mindedness, logic, and prudence.

Strong critical thinking skills and high emotional intelligence work well together. However, the exclusion of one is likely a detriment to the other.

✅ The Well of Five Whys

To get to the root cause of a problem, start with a simple fact. Then, go deeper into the well by continuing to ask "why" after each answer for a total of five times.

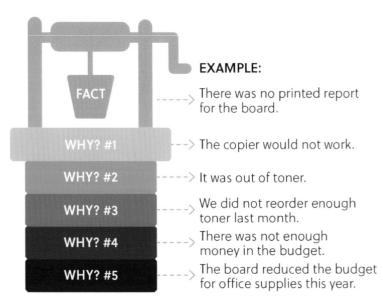

EXAMPLE:

FACT ----> There was no printed report for the board.

WHY? #1 --> The copier would not work.

WHY? #2 ----> It was out of toner.

WHY? #3 ----> We did not reorder enough toner last month.

WHY? #4 ----> There was not enough money in the budget.

WHY? #5 ----> The board reduced the budget for office supplies this year.

18 Characteristics of Strong Critical Thinking Skills

1. Inquisitive, asks well-formulated questions, and seeks truth, accuracy, and fairness.

2. Willing to scrutinize one's own motives and assumptions.

3. Strives to be free of prejudice, bias, and self-deception.

4. Practices self-correction, humility, and integrity.

5. Investigates the correlation between theory and practice.

6. Identifies information distortion or propaganda.

7. Uses a systematic approach to problem-solving.

8. Formulates practical solutions fitting the context.

9. Observes and interprets the context correctly.

10. Understands the importance of prioritization.

11. Sorts and scores pertinent information.

12. Recognizes unstated assumptions and values.

13. Forms concrete thoughts from vague or abstract concepts.

14. Autonomous – not unduly influenced by the thinking of others.

15. Reduces complexity and brings clarity.

16. Comprehends obstacles to effectiveness.

17. Maintains objectivity.

18. Consistently delivers well-reasoned conclusions and solutions.

Critical Thinker Vs. Critical Person

There is often a fine line yet big difference between a person who thinks critically and a person who is critical. The following infographic explains how you can tell the difference and how you can adjust your actions to be a critical thinker.

WHICH ARE YOU?
CRITICAL THINKER VS. CRITICAL PERSON

Asks questions to learn		Asks questions to embarrass
Looks at things from different perspectives		Looks at things from one perspective – their own!
Contributes to solutions		Contributes to problems
Generates ideas		Critiques ideas
Rewards risk-taking and experimentation		Hinders risk-taking and experimentation
Welcomes questions of their ideas		Questions others but does not like being questioned
Contributes to hope and innovation		Contributes to fear and low morale

Decide How to Decide

Knowing in advance WHO will make a decision and HOW the decision will be made is critical to sound decision making.

Types of Decision-Making

- **Decision by an individual:** This may be an owner, manager, or staff member.

- **Decision by a small group:** This is most often a work team, management team, or board.

- **Decision by unanimous consent:** This is when more than one person is involved in the decision, and either they want agreement or the by-laws require it.

- **Decision by a popular majority:** This is when you must have either a simple majority of 51% or more or a supermajority such as two-thirds or three-quarters.

    It does not mean that everyone agrees, but it does mean that everyone agrees to implement a decision because they believe their reservations and concerns were heard and considered, resulting in a decision that is best under the circumstances.

> Clarifying and articulating decision rights is often the first order of business in fixing a passive-aggressive organization, where decisions have been made, unmade, overturned, and second-guessed so many times that no one really knows who truly decides what anymore.
>
> *– Gary Neilson, Bruce Pasternack,*
> *and Karen Van Nuys*
> *"The Passive-Aggressive Organization"*
> *Harvard Business Review, 2005*

How to Make a Good Decision: It Takes More Than Agreement

A group makes a unanimous decision regarding who to hire, yet the hire ends up being an epic failure. A leader makes a decision that goes against the will of the group, yet it ends up being a home run decision. Managing the quality of a decision and the quality of team cohesion is no easy task for any leader. This framework will help you understand the balancing act between agreement and accuracy.

1. High Agreement/Low Accuracy

On more than one occasion, I have either watched or been an active part of a group decision where there was strong agreement among the members, but it turned out to be a poor decision. One example was regarding who to hire. Everyone

High level of agreement & a bad decision

High level of agreement & a good decision

Low level of agreement & a bad decision

Low level of agreement & a good decision

AGREEMENT

ACCURACY

agreed on the candidate, but once hired, that candidate was not successful and was eventually let go. Sometimes we can confuse high agreement with an accurate decision. The power of groupthink as well as the fear of disagreement can result in a perceived high agreement decision that has poor outcomes. (Although high agreement can sometimes mean an accurate decision, but not in every case.)

If this is your situation: Make sure you are not experiencing groupthink by inviting honesty and safety for questions and disagreement. This can be accomplished using anonymous feedback tools as well as external facilitators to help you make sure you are getting accurate information.

2. Low Agreement/Low Accuracy

What happens when you mix a group that is not unified on a decision with a decision that goes bad? Blame and conflict! Some will blame the leader for making the decision without having enough group support, while the leader(s) will blame the group members for being obstructionists and difficult. We experienced this many years ago when assisting a client that had almost no agreement among themselves. When a decision was finally made that was less than perfect, even more conflict arose among some members. While having low group support may be a reason for a failed decision, we also know that decisions can fail even with strong support if you do not have accuracy.

If this is your situation: Consider getting help to assess why you are experiencing such low agreement and poor decisions. Seek to discover if it is an issue of the team's dynamics, the leader's style, or the culture within the team or organization.

3. High Accuracy/Low Agreement

The son of a world-renowned science researcher became severely ill. For years, many similar patients were told it was in their head and there was no biological cause for how they were feeling. Even though there was low agreement among the medical community, this researcher set out to find the cause and eventually did! There are times when a leader believes he knows what needs to be done – who to hire, what product or program to launch, or what event to host – and takes the risk of pushing through the group. While very risky, some of the most profound decisions in history came about this way.

If this is your situation: Assess why you are high in your decision accuracy but the team is not able to agree. Are they in conflict with each other, with you, or with the mission?

4. High Accuracy/High Agreement

Whether you are buying stock, hiring an employee, or starting a new business, a good decision requires being accurate in your knowledge of what your options are and why one choice is better than the others. Having honest input from others also increases the likelihood of making a good choice, and it adds to the culture and chemistry of the team. While it is not always possible to attain, a decision that involves high accuracy with high team agreement is worthy of pursuit. It will provide the most input, a sense of shared ownership, an increased likelihood of a good choice, and a sense of accomplishment.

If this is your situation: Consider celebrating as well as protecting. It is not easy to attain consistently high accuracy in decisions with high agreement among your team, so celebrate the "wins." Additionally, learn more about what is contributing to this healthy synergy and protect it from disruption.

5 Elements of Discernment

Unilateral decisions made without counsel can often be void of discernment. Include the following five elements in the process to increase the likelihood of making good decisions relative to the values and direction of your organization.

Critical Thinking
Create a safe environment for your advisors to ask hard questions and test assumptions.

Respect
Show appreciation for the value each person brings to the discussion.

Counsel
Believe others have knowledge, skills, and life experiences that can aid you in making decisions.

5 ELEMENTS OF DISCERNMENT

Confidentiality
Guard confidentiality by deciding what information, if any, will be shared outside of the meeting.

Honesty
To overcome self-delusion and confirmation, insist on brutal honesty and verifiable facts.

"Plans fail for lack of counsel, but with many advisors they succeed." –Proverbs 15:22

10 Traps to Avoid to Make Better Decisions

No organization or leader makes perfect decisions all the time. But during critical points, one bad decision can cause catastrophic failure. If you want to make better decisions, avoid the following 10 traps. Which trap do you gravitate towards?

1. Holding too high of an opinion of yourself.

The results of viewing ourselves as "greater than we are" are the same: acting over-confidently, failing to seek advice, assuming we are smarter than we are, and ultimately, a whole lot of damage!

2. Failing to seek or listen to wise counsel.

Leaders often can make important decisions, decisions that can have a significant impact on themselves and those whom they serve, with little or no counsel. The technical term for this person is "fool"!

3. Making decisions impulsively.

One major reason to avoid making decisions impulsively is that "when considering a decision, the mind gives disproportionate weight to the first information it receives. Initial impressions, estimates, or data anchor subsequent thoughts and judgments," according to John S. Hammond, Ralph L. Keeney, and Howard Raiffa in "The Hidden Traps in Decision Making," *Harvard Business Review*, 2006.

4. Allowing the search for a "perfect" decision to create paralysis.

The fear of a mistake can incapacitate us. It is admirable to desire to make a good decision, but it is often a lack of courage when we seek a perfect one. Paralysis when making a hard decision can also be due to a fear of conflict. While there are times when waiting longer is appropriate, this can also be a sign of a leader, board, or team living in fear and avoiding any risks.

5. Facing a decision that exceeds the skills or mental/emotional capacity of the leadership.

Leaders may face a decision that exceeds their mental or emotional capacity, and quite often, they can face a number of such decisions all at once. Just as for trap #2, leaders need to surround themselves with others who have experience and can help shed clarity on the situation.

6. Viewing questions as an enemy rather than a friend.

On many occasions, we have seen how a leader can become aggressive or defensive when questioned. Yet, without being questioned, a leader is much more likely to make poor decisions since he or she may not have thought it through or missed important information that could have improved the decision or prevented a damaging decision from being made.

7. Failing to understand and manage human/group dynamics.

According to Dr. Daniel Goleman, one of the leading researchers in emotional intelligence, groups often tend to make better decisions than individuals, but this is usually true only when the group has a high level of trust and healthy group dynamics. Research has shown that if we have experienced a negative emotion, like anger, close in time to when we are making a decision, that emotion may influence our approach to the decision even though the two were unrelated.

8. Spiritualizing decisions.

One of the tempting ways for Christian leaders to respond to confusion and complexity is to spiritualize the problem or decision. While all decisions have a spiritual aspect, spiritualization often occurs when a sound decision-making process is eliminated. Spiritualization artificially simplifies challenges and seldom leads to wise decisions. Ultimately, it abuses and trivializes God and His Word.

9. Failing to correct a bad decision.

More often than not, when we feel like we may have made a bad decision, we continue moving ahead instead of correcting the decision.

10. Succumbing to decision overload.

The average person today is being confronted with an ever-increasing amount of responsibility and information (aka information overload). In his book *Paradox of Choice* (2016), Dr. Barry Schwartz notes that while freedom to choose is a good thing, too many options can incapacitate a person's ability to make a decision.

> Get wisdom, get understanding; do not forget my words or swerve from them. Do not forsake wisdom, and she will protect you; love her, and she will watch over you. Wisdom is supreme; therefore get wisdom. Though it cost all you have, get understanding.
>
> – Proverbs 4:5-7

 **Decision Lanes**

Most governance-related conflict occurs because there is a lack of clarity or lack of agreement about who has the final authority to make which decisions. Use the Decision Lanes Chart to predetermine who has decision rights and any limitations placed on the decision-maker(s). When you cross over lanes, there will be a collision. The damages can be significant organizationally and relationally. The Decision Lanes Chart below provides some hypothetical examples. Create new examples of likely decisions and move them to the correct column for your organization's context. When a decision is to be made, the decision-maker(s) should let others know if they planning to:

1. Just give an **FYI** when the decision is made.

2. Ask for **INPUT** before making the decision.

3. Let others give their **APPROVAL**.

SAMPLE DECISION LANES CHART

Create new examples of likely decisions and move them to the correct column for your organization's context.

Full Board	Executive Team	CEO	Stakeholders
Official policies	Board agenda	Day-to-day operations	Major merger
Accountability for the CEO	Propose budget items	Hire/dismiss staff	Hiring a CEO

✅ The Decision-Making Grids

For simple, less complex, personal decisions, the "Eisenhower Matrix" can be helpful.

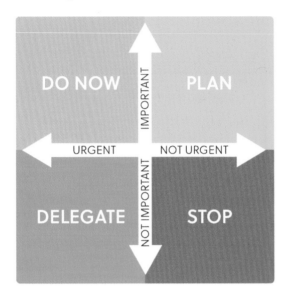

For complex decisions, a weighted grid of questions like the following sample can help you evaluate the impact of specific decisions. Often, unintended consequences occur because key questions were not considered.

Using the following chart, create your own grid to properly weigh the significance of key decisions. The questions and scoring will be different for each organization. Solid decisions should have a 70% certainty rate, especially when the decision(s) will require a significant amount of change within the organization. For ease of calculation, weights are based on a possible score of 100.

SAMPLE WEIGHTED DECISION-MAKING GRID

Customize the questions and weight factors
BEFORE making complex decisions.

Questions to Consider: "Will this decision..."	"Yes" Weight Factor	Mark "x" if "Yes"	Score
...advance the stated mission of the organization?	10	x	10
...align with our current priorities?	5	x	5
...be widely accepted with our constituency or customers?	5	-	-
...correct a current problem/inefficiency?	10	x	10
...have strong support from the staff?	5	x	5
...have strong support from key influencers?	5	-	-
...set a positive precedence for the future?	5	x	5
...increase income to the organization?	10	x	10
...increase our capacity to serve our customers?	5	-	-
Add your own questions & assign weights			
	10	x	10
	5	x	5
	10	x	10
	5	x	5
	10	-	-
Total	100		75

Likelihood of Success:

0-59%	60-74%	75-100%
Poor	Moderate	Good

We must discipline ourselves to be available –
physically and emotionally – to one another ... (Most)
relationships feel like intrusions or interruptions
instead of being enjoyed as gifts or, even more, being
celebrated as one of life's highest purposes.

DOUGLAS RUMFORD

CHAPTER FIVE

Emotional & Relational Growth

10 Questions for Emotional & Relational Management

One of the most common reasons an organization transitions an employee is his or her inability to manage emotions or relationships with others. The following questions will help you better understand and manage yourself emotionally and relationally. As you consider each question, also ask yourself, "How do I know this is true?"

1. Research shows effective leaders spend 80-90% of their time in connection with others. How much time do you spend building relationships with those around you?

2. Do you find that those around you are more often attracted to you or repelled by you?

3. Everyone has blind spots. Do you know yours? What are your methods of acquiring feedback?

4. Are you viewed by others as relationally engaging or socially distant? How do you know?

5. As a leader, do you most often depend upon telling (positional) or influencing (relational)?

6. Are you known for working towards mutual agreement or always having to get your way?

7. Would those around you describe you as someone who listens and empathizes with others?

8. Are you known for understanding and controlling your emotions?

9. Do those you work with enjoy working with you?

10. Do you help those around you to monitor and manage their relational and emotional health?

Note: One of the best ways to identify and correct potential blind spots is by acquiring anonymous feedback from those around you which can be done by utilizing a professionally facilitated 360° feedback process.

11 Actions That Build Healthy Relationships in the Workplace

1. HONOR those who deserve honor.
2. GREET others respectfully.
3. ENCOURAGE those you interact with.
4. SUBMIT to those in authority.
5. Exercise PATIENCE.
6. Show genuine INTEREST.
7. PRAISE honestly and freely.
8. Speak TRUTHFULLY.
9. Practice KINDNESS.
10. SUPPORT & ASSIST others.
11. Practice TOLERANCE whenever possible and appropriate.

> Confrontation is a precious gift. When it is withheld, teams deteriorate, performances fail, families break apart, and companies go bankrupt. The lack of appropriate, effective confrontation is fatal to communities, and it can be lethal to individual men and women.
>
> – *John Ortberg*

Understanding & Managing Relationships

When conflict occurs, we need to know what corner to head towards. This chart explains several important dynamics to be mindful of as you prepare for conflict resolution. In conflict, we want to show BOTH high value for the relationship AND address the needs we have personally. This is especially true if the conflict includes personal attacks.

I MUST WIN

These individuals do not value the relationship, and their ego drives their need to "win" in the conflict regardless of the cost to others. Controlling is essential to these self-serving individuals who believe the organization exists to serve them. They make life difficult for others until they get their way. This profile fits the immature leader, the narcissistic boss, or the domineering spouse.

I YIELD TO YOU

These individuals highly value the relationship and will relinquish their own needs and desires to maintain the relationship. A person with this profile is likely to feel insecure in their relationships or in their job. They may be enamored with the "strong leader" type or simply be a highly compliant person even though this corner leaves them feeling unfulfilled in the long term.

I QUIT / WITHDRAW

When the conflict reaches a certain point, these individuals will withdraw and head for the door. They will easily abandon the relationship and their responsibilities because they find little satisfaction in them and do not value them. They often have a lack of passion for the mission and organization. They are in the classic lose-lose situation.

I RESOLVE

When personal needs are being met (high) and the value of the relationship increases (high), the very process of resolving conflict makes you a better person, and your team or family reaps the benefits. Win-win happens best when this corner is chosen in advance. Understand it requires compromise, openness, and integrity to get there. High emotional intelligence enables this person to thrive in most organizations.

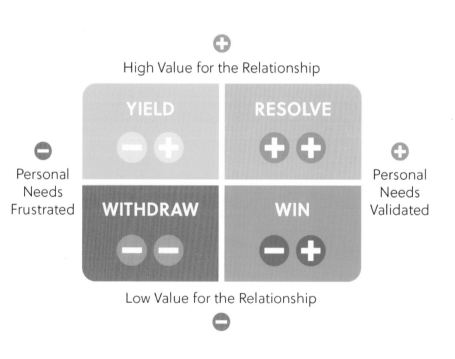

"Conflict is inevitable, but combat is optional."

– *Max Lucado*

12 Ways to Improve Your Relational Dynamics

1. Regularly seek feedback from those who know you well.

2. Seek to learn more by reading about emotional intelligence and relational management.

3. Set a few specific goals for the purpose of growing in this area of your life.

4. Identify and learn from people who model good emotional and relational management.

5. Consider doing a professionally facilitated 360° feedback assessment.

6. When feeling threatened or embarrassed, resist blaming, avoiding, or withdrawing.

7. Prepare for and practice responding in a healthy manner, especially in anticipation of difficult meetings or interactions.

8. Quickly work to ensure an organizational disagreement does not become a deep-seated personal conflict.

9. Before speaking, sending an email or text, or posting online, always take the appropriate time to ask yourself, "Will I regret this later?"

10. When working on changing behaviors, seek feedback from people who are observing you in that context.

11. Intentionally spend informal time with your coworkers listening, learning, and showing interest.

12. When needed, consider seeking a professional coach to help you grow in this area.

9 Things Successful People Think About Themselves

Success is not just about what we do, it starts with how we think. From the complex study of neuroscience to what every experienced leader has observed, those who lead successfully over the long-haul model certain thought practices. Even the Bible places special emphasis on the power of what we think including, "As he thinks within himself, so he is," Proverbs 23:7 and, "Think about what is noble and right," Philippians 4:8. Here are nine things successful people commonly think about themselves, and you should too.

1. I am stronger than I think.

Successful leaders experience setbacks and suffering like everyone else. The one difference is that in the midst of hardship such as illness, divorce, loss of a key customer or employee, bankruptcy, etc., they remind themselves that they have made it through other setbacks and they will get through this one too.

2. I am not irreplaceable.

Let's face it, deep down many leaders and managers feel like they cannot be replaced. But successful ones know better. They know that while they may be important or even vital to the organization, there were others before them who left, retired, or died, and the organization continued on just fine, and in some cases even better (which can be a bit humbling).

3. I am capable of more than what I presently do.

Mediocre leaders have a tendency to start coasting. But just like a professional athlete, top leaders challenge themselves to reach an even higher level. Coasting is not an option and is not even in their vocabulary. They push themselves to grow, keep learning, take on new challenges, overcome the obstacles in front of them, and then go even further.

4. I focus more on being grateful for what I have than on what I do not.

Successful leaders have a regular spirit of gratitude. Rather than focusing on what is missing, they acknowledge and appreciate what they do have including the sacrifices others make for them, the gifts God has given to them, the successes they have experienced, and the relationships that support them.

5. I am sure I have blind spots, and I genuinely want to know what they are.

Yes, not only do the most successful leaders have limited sight in how they act, but they also sometimes have BIG blind spots. That is not a shocker. We all do. But what is surprising is how successful leaders can be self-aware by humbly acknowledging that they have blind spots, seeking to learn from others to grow through the blind spots, and learning to manage the damage they can cause.

6. I may be important, but I am not the only important person in the room.

The more successful a leader becomes, the more they are at risk for pride and narcissism. Yet, the most successful leaders long-term are those who genuinely believe that there are plenty of important people on the team besides themselves.

7. I focus more on what can be done and how than on what cannot be done and why.

Can you imagine if Jeff Bezos said it is impossible to deliver a package in less than 48 hours, or if Elon Musk said you can't get to space any cheaper? Of course not! That's because successful leaders focus on what can be done and find a way to do it. Their vision to do something significant is greater than their fear of failing.

8. I highly value accomplishments, but I value relationships even more.

Many leaders have experienced success while stepping on or over a trainload of other people. But leaders with a deeper definition of success are those who can look in a mirror at the end of their lives and feel good with not only the WHAT but also the WHO.

9. I am so much more than my greatest mistake or my biggest success.

Successful leaders are great at keeping both their successes in perspective as well as their failures. Neither our biggest success nor our most embarrassing failure is a complete picture of who we are as a leader. And leaders who are successful over the long term know this and work to continually remind themselves of it.

10 Tips for Giving & Receiving Feedback

1. Feedback is wanted and needed.

One of the top complaints from both volunteers and employees is that they receive too little feedback on how they are doing. Performance is directly linked to setting clear expectations and then providing ongoing feedback that is direct, specific, and non-punishing.

2. Feedback should be authentic.

Each person is wired differently. This means our feedback should affirm strengths and talents as well as identify blind spots that may cause harm to the individual or the organization.

3. Feedback should be two-way and ongoing, resulting in few surprises.

If a person is surprised, that means they have not heard the feedback or it has not been shared with them.

4. People are different, so the coaching that is provided and the way the feedback is given should be customized.

Some need feedback that is firm and even confrontational. Others only need a gentle reminder. Be sure to give feedback in a way that will be best for that person.

5. We have a tendency to avoid conversations that may be difficult.

Remember, avoiding performance problems too long will lower morale and performance.

6. Timing of the feedback matters.

Feedback that comes close in time to when the recipient did something exceptional is often fruitful, yet that which comes close to a performance error may be less effective. It is not wise to give hard feedback when the recipient may not have the capacity to receive and process it.

7. Whether you are giving or receiving feedback, expect defensiveness and discouragement.

Defensiveness and discouragement are part of hearing critical feedback, especially if the feedback conflicts with the person's perception of self.

8. Relationship matters.

Feedback is best received when it comes from someone who is trusted and has a good relationship with the recipient.

9. Don't over-respond.

People tend to overreact or fixate on selective comments. A leader should not be too quick to change behavior every time someone expresses criticism or affirmation. Rather, a leader should reflect upon the feedback and, with the assistance of a wise coach or supervisor, determine if a change is appropriate.

10. Leaders with positional power should be discerning of both compliments and critiques.

People who hold positional power should remember that those who compliment may have other motives. In addition, leaders should add additional "volume" to those who give mild critique. People will often ratchet down the intensity of what they feel due to fear of conflict.

7 Actions That Complement Emotional Intelligence

It makes a huge difference when leaders have good self-awareness and manage their emotions and relationships well. However, just emotional intelligence (EQ) is NOT ENOUGH! I have met plenty of leaders who are caring, thoughtful, sensitive to the needs of others, and well-liked by others, yet they are not succeeding in their leadership roles. Although there are many differences between successful leaders, they have these seven things in common beyond EQ. Successful leaders...

1. Possess a passion for the vision
They are excited about what they are aiming to accomplish.

2. Are fanatically focused
They never drift from their pursuit of the vision.

3. Work harder than others
They are not only not afraid of hard work, they love it.

4. Attract talent
They attract talented leaders because of their vision and passion.

5. Take calculated risks
They take plenty of risks but are seldom reckless.

6. Possess the gift of disruption
They know how to disrupt the norm to create the new.

7. Are decisive decision-makers
They lean towards imperfect decisions over no decisions.

20 Ways to Encourage Others

1. Know what motivates the individual (time off, monetary incentives, opportunity) and provide it.

2. Catch people doing something good and immediately tell them.

3. Hand-deliver a "goodie" to someone's office/desk.

4. Send an encouraging email, text message, or note.

5. Provide a small gift of appreciation.

6. Tell someone something that you appreciate about him/her.

7. In the presence of others, identify a unique contribution he/she makes to your organization.

8. Share an appropriate joke with someone.

9. Show genuine interest in the interests of others.

10. When appropriate, treat someone to a meal.

11. Provide resources and information to help people in areas of personal interest or professional expertise.

12. Invite someone's input or ideas.

13. Tell someone as they are about to leave on vacation that the vacation is well-deserved.

14. Offer to provide tangible, practical help in time of need.

15. Recognize significant occasions/anniversaries (work tenure, birthdays, etc.).

16. Offer to perform a job-related task for someone when unexpected circumstances arise.

17. When appropriate, spend social time together.

18. Promote a sense of value and respect within the organization.

19. Practice random acts of kindness.

20. No matter what you say or do, be sincere and accurate.

I have yet to find the man, however exalted his station, who did not do better work and put forth greater effort under a spirit of approval than under a spirit of criticism.

– Charles Schwab

Conflict Strategies

NEGOTIATE
I Win / You Win
What can I give up in order to get what I feel I need most to function well?

CAPITULATE
I Lose / You Win
Fearing reprisal, embarrassment, or the inadequacies in my view, I surrender my way to yours.

DOMINATE
I Win / You Lose
Believing there is no room for compromise on the issue, I must demonstrate that my way is superior to yours.

17 Questions to Ask Yourself in Conflict

1. What/who do I believe is the primary source of the conflict?

2. Is this a disagreement or is divisiveness present?

3. What has actually been lost in the conflict so far?

4. Am I personally a part of the conflict?

5. Is the conflict involving staff members or programs of this organization?

6. Does this conflict put the organization at risk?

7. Who else should be informed about this conflict?

8. What should be my role, if any, at this time?

9. Is there a conflict of interest present by anyone representing the organization?

10. Do I have any legal responsibilities as a result of this conflict?

11. Is anyone in danger?

12. Are there well-established principles that are being overtly violated?

13. Is the conflict simple or complex?

14. Is there a sense of violation of absolutes, convictions, or preferences?

15. Should outside, expert help be sought, and, if so, what kind of help?

16. Is there a long-term pattern of conflict?

17. What are the next 3-5 steps that should be taken?

✅ Blameless Resolution

Conflict is normal and healthy if all parties show humility, grace, and forgiveness. Conflict can also be destructive to others personally as well as highly disruptive to the productivity and performance of the organization.

Practice "blameless resolution." It is blameless because everyone tries to quickly own their mistakes, errors in judgment, and attitudes that hinder the work. In other words, there is no need to "blame" someone who already "owns it" and is correcting the problem. In return, we expect those on the team to model the maturity to resolve conflicts privately, confidentially, and completely. Failure to do so will insipidly creep into the organization in the form of gossip, slander, libel, or demeaning comments or actions. The desired healthy culture of the organization will suffer.

> "Conflict is the gadfly of thought. It stirs us to observation and memory. It instigates to invention. It shocks us out of sheep-like passivity, and sets us at noting and contriving... conflict is a sine qua non of [essential to] reflection and ingenuity."
>
> – John Dewey

CHAPTER SIX

Change & Momentum

There's a way to do it better – find it.

THOMAS EDISON

8 Actions of a Smart Change Leader

Credible Leaders
Those who are viewed as trustworthy and proven

Compelling Vision
An inspiring picture that instills hope for the future

Wise Counsel
Skilled, objective truth-tellers to test your thinking

Champions
75% of key players believe in it and own it

Good Timing
People do not have unlimited capacity for change

Significant Communication
When you think you've said it enough, say it again

Effective Execution
Timely, well-planned implementation

Humility
Willingness to make corrections and even abandon the initiative

 10 Questions to Ask Before Launching a Change

1. What is the risk to the organization by either making or not making this change?

2. What is the timing of this change within the organization?

3. What is the resistance that is expected if this change is implemented versus not implemented?

4. What is the perceived credibility level of the person/group proposing the change?

5. Is there a compelling vision for this change?

6. Is there a clear communication plan for explaining the change?

7. Have the systemic effects of the change on the organization been considered?

8. What is the level of leadership agreement regarding the change?

9. Has the proposed change been tested in an environment of honest dialogue?

10. Is there a well-designed plan in place to implement the proposed change?

> During times of uncertainty and change, leaders do not need to have all the answers, but they would be wise to be accessible, to communicate often, and to seek wise counsel.
>
> *– Jay Desko, Ph.D.*

✔ The Cycle of Resistance

We have a change
we want to make.

We push even
harder or... we
give up.

We share our
"facts."

They find more
reasons and
ways to resist.

Resistance
emerges.

We then move
from "facts" to
"fear."

Confirmation bias
"proves" they are
right.

Resistance often emerges due to:

Low credibility
Past failures of change
Limited emotional capacity
Fear of losing position or status
Belief it is a bad idea

✓ 11 Ways to Communicate Change

1. Strive to connect the change to the vision and values.

2. Specify the nature of the change and honestly explain why.

3. Share the complete picture even if it is bad news.

4. Repeat often the purpose of the change and the actions planned.

5. Create opportunities for feedback and listening not just "selling."

6. Seek to have senior staff onboard before initiation.

7. Show and celebrate progress.

8. Create a common message and language for the change.

9. Simplify and reduce the different messages communicated.

10. Utilize multiple means of communication, especially face-to-face.

11. Model the change yourself.

3 Elements of Momentum

Many factors play into organizational momentum including God's choosing to do something big or special despite the leaders or circumstances. However, that is more often the exception than the rule. From our consulting experience, three elements are present in high momentum organizations. When you have the convergence of credible leaders, compelling vision, and effective execution, a powerful and positive reaction takes place that results in attracting great talent, financial donations, and investing.

1. Credible Leaders

Credible leaders are those who are viewed as trustworthy and proven. These are leaders who employees, followers, and donors believe can and will do the right things and do things right.

2. Compelling Vision

Often referred to as a preferred future, a compelling vision is a short descriptive picture of what your organization is aiming for. While leaders cannot control the context, they can collaboratively dream of new ways to serve others, solve problems, and impact lives. Such a vision is inspiring yet attainable.

3. Effective Execution

One of the unfortunate and unnecessary ways leaders harm their credibility and the momentum of their organization is by not ensuring that a decision or plan, for which they are responsible, is carried out in a timely manner. In their book *Execution, The Discipline of Getting Things Done* (2002), Larry

Bossidy and Ram Charan note that execution is the major job of a leader, and it must be a key element of the organization's culture. No matter how compelling the vision, it is irrelevant if action is not taken.

Compelling Vision
A short, inspiring picture of your organization's future.

Credible Leaders
Those who are viewed as trustworthy and proven.

Momentum

Effective Execution
Timely, well-planned implementation.

 **6 Momentum Killers**

1. Too much talk, too little action.

2. Too many voices are involved.

3. Too complex a planning process.

4. Too much confusion over roles.

5. Too much fear of risk.

6. Too much confidence.

9 Ways to Build & Sustain Vision & Momentum

1. Protect the organization from you!

The fears, insecurities, ego needs, and arrogance of one or more leaders can be the single greatest harm to a high-momentum organization.

2. Build a great leadership environment and team.

A blend of catalysts, experts, and testers working in a high-trust environment can do amazing things!

3. Face your organization's reality; don't avoid it.

Every organization has ups and downs. However, an organization cannot improve until it honestly faces its weaknesses and opportunities.

4. Swing for singles, enjoy home runs.

Many organizations strive for home runs. However, most momentum comes from the convergence of small opportunities, small actions, and small successes over a long period.

5. Compare your organization to your vision, not to others.

Comparison can be deadly to momentum. Other organizations are not your measure – your vision is.

6. Experiment when you are strong.

The best time to try new ideas for momentum is when the organization is healthy, having both energy and resources. Even when an organization is weak, however, it must still experiment. Not experimenting will likely lead to further decline.

7. If everyone is talking about it, think twice about doing it.

Often, organizations adopt programs and events because so many others do. Sustainable momentum is seldom built this way.

8. Guard momentum since it is hard to acquire and easy to lose.

It only takes a few hurtful events or bad decisions to lose it.

9. Remember that success is often a greater enemy than being average.

When an organization is experiencing momentum, its leaders can become proud, resulting in arrogance and the failure to continue learning.

Momentum Markers

POSITIVE MOMENTUM	VS	NEGATIVE MOMENTUM
Can do no wrong	1	Can do no right
Infectious optimism	2	Growing cynicism
Increasing credibility	3	Decreasing credibility
Confidence & celebration	4	Fear & defeat
Sense of voice & ownership	5	Control & forced "positivism"
Positive numbers & outcomes	6	Negative numbers & outcomes

9 Ways to Assess Momentum

1. Don't ignore intuition.
Do you have a growing sense that great things are happening?

2. Gather feedback from your staff and board.
Are they unified, passionate, and engaged?

3. Money follows momentum.
Are major gifts and regular giving on the increase or decrease?

4. Look at the fruit.
Is there unquestionable evidence of life change in those you serve?

5. Look at your vision and priorities.
Are they clear and compelling, and are people unified around them?

6. Look at your calendar.
Does it reflect new and energizing initiatives?

7. Get the pulse of those you serve.
Are they raving supporters: inviting, serving, and giving?

8. Assess employee longevity and commitment.
Are you attracting and retaining people who are passionate about the organization?

9. Consider who you hire.
Are you attracting highly talented staff?

4 Seasons of Organizational Health

Every organization has seasons of dysfunction. The more aware you are of this dysfunction, the more you can intentionally seek to address and correct it. It is wise for leaders to regularly look at the present season of health in the organization and seek the perspectives of board members, employees, and/or volunteers. The four seasons also apply to our personal lives as well.

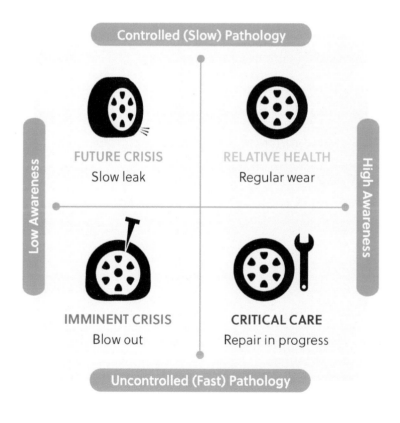

9 "Change Mistakes" That Compromise Organizational Health

1. Making too many changes too quickly.

2. Making changes too little too late.

3. Undiscussed issues and faulty assumptions.

4. Sense of contentment and risk aversion.

5. Vilifying those who resist.

6. Low trust and credibility environment.

7. Too few courageous champions.

8. Inadequate communication.

9. Misplaced identity on the "life cycle."

The Life Cycle of an Organization

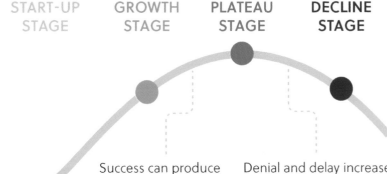

START-UP STAGE	GROWTH STAGE	PLATEAU STAGE	DECLINE STAGE

Success can produce pride and over confidence resulting in feelings of invincibility and complacency.

Denial and delay increase risk and decrease the likelihood of making the changes essential for the future health.

CHAPTER SEVEN

Teamwork & Supervision

Coming together is a beginning; keeping together is progress; working together is success.

HENRY FORD

4 Elements in Coaching Others

1. Goals of Coaching

- Preventing problems before they emerge.
- Correcting problems that have already emerged.
- Directing the person toward a positive destination.

2. Stages of Coaching

- Listening in order to gain understanding.
- Prioritizing goals to be pursued.
- Implementing actions towards agreed-upon goals.

3. Approaches to Coaching

- Encouraging the heart.
- Teaching the skills necessary for success.
- Confronting unhealthy behaviors.

4. Tools of Coaching

- Feedback using input from those who serve with the person.
- Meeting regularly to coach the person.
- Goals to help the person proactively move forward.

✓ The Coaching Mountain

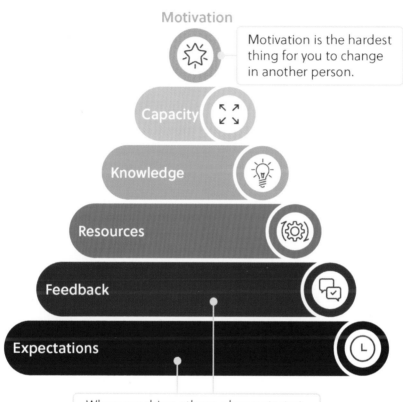

Motivation

Motivation is the hardest thing for you to change in another person.

Capacity

Knowledge

Resources

Feedback

Expectations

When coaching others, always start at the bottom of the coaching mountain. It is your place of greatest influence.

5 Reminders About Effective Teams

1. Leaders set the tone for the team.

Research continues to demonstrate that strong relational connection is a significant predictor of team success. In their book, *Primal Leadership: Learning to Lead with Emotional Intelligence*, researchers Daniel Goleman, Richard E. Boyatzis, and Annie McKee stress that the absence of relational harmony often results in reduced decision-making speed and quality. They emphasize that it is the leaders who must take responsibility for the relational tone of the team, meetings, and hope for the future.

2. Team conflict is normal.

It is both normal and healthy for teams to go through a season of turbulence and conflict. Conflict can and does take place even among the most mature and faithful leaders. There is significant research that demonstrates it is not as much the conflict that breaks a relationship as it is the ratio of negative versus positive interactions. Relationships that have at least four or five positive interactions for every negative one are more likely to retain the relationship. When a team successfully navigates such seasons, it will be stronger and have a better opportunity to both model and train others with wisdom and hope.

3. Team cohesion is essential.

Well-intentioned, highly-skilled, hard-working, rightly-motivated people CANNOT guarantee that a team will function well together. They need "relational glue" to make it work. Emotional intelligence factors are among the most significant reasons why teams succeed or fail. Relationships are one of the pillars of trust and team health. Strong team cohesion serves as a firewall against divisive people and the dilution of vision. Cracks in cohesion increase the likelihood for pathogens to take up residence in a team, resulting in "disease" which infects the team and can spread far and wide.

4. Leaders are often slow to seek help.

Pride. Embarrassment. Loyalty. Job security. There are many reasons why we are sometimes slow to seek help. However, if the relational dynamics do not improve and help is not sought, leaders have to find ways to alleviate the discomfort and make sense of it all. This usually involves a combination of avoidance, blaming, vilifying the "enemy," and finding others who support their position. The longer it goes on, the harder it is to ever return to a healthy and effective level of team performance.

5. Relational damage is hard to repair.

When team cohesion deteriorates, it is hard to rebuild, and when it deteriorates to a very low level, it seldom can be recovered. Trust is the confidence that someone will meet our expectations. Trust is much harder to cultivate than it is to lose.

6 Characteristics of Teams That Get Results

Every effective team needs the right elements to be successful. The following list includes the top six characteristics of high-performing teams. Teams that get results…

1. Share Vision

A team that gets results always has a shared vision and shared priorities. While each person may not agree on every nuance, this shared vision unifies them and provides a focus for their energy.

2. Love Work

If you absolutely love 75% or more of what you do, you will feel less stress, complain less about your job, and wake up energized to get to it. Team members who love their work add great value.

3. Work Hard

One team member that does not work hard can negatively impact the morale and performance of the whole team.

4. Stay Sharp

Your value to the team is influenced by how well you stay on top of your professional skills. Research has shown that experts, or those who are the best of the best, are four times as productive as an average member of the team.

5. Communicate Often

We may feel we have shared the right information in the right volume, but we often forget that people are overwhelmed with messages and most people are not very good at listening! Communication helps build and maintain shared understanding and trust.

6. Relate Well

The foundation for any strong relationship is trust and respect, and it is critical that a team relates well to one another. It requires intentional effort to create trust, and it requires almost no effort to lose it!

Am I in the Right Seat?

First who, then what. "Get the right people on the bus" is a concept developed in the book *Good to Great* by Jim Collins. Those who build great organizations make sure they have the right people on the bus and the right people in the key seats before they figure out where to drive the bus. Are you in the right seat? Things change and people change. Over time, you can find yourself in the wrong seat. Ask yourself these three questions to find your "sweet spot."

9 Signs of a Healthy Team

1. Increasing joy, fun, and celebration among leaders.

2. Increasing sense of "we" especially among staff and leadership/board.

3. Increasing time spent together relationally beyond meetings and tasks.

4. Increasing recruitment and retention of exceptional staff moving forward.

5. Increasing confidence and follow-through regarding decisions.

6. Increasing honesty in discussing previously undiscussed issues.

7. Increasing sense of momentum within the team.

8. Increasing trust and confidence among one another.

9. Increasing cohesion around a shared vision.

Office Drama & How to Tame It

The workplace is made up of people, and with people naturally comes quirks, jerks, and… drama. The most common ingredients of workplace drama are gossip, jealousy, cliques, and secrets. While office drama is common, at its worst, it can be harmful to employees' spirits resulting in added stress, more missed days, and higher turnover. The damage can even go beyond the employees to the actual mission of the organization. And, contrary to popular stereotypes, there are just as many drama kings as there are queens. Here are seven ways to help tame the drama in your office or workplace.

1. Some drama is normal, so be realistic.

Remember, we have all earned our place on the island of misfit people. We are imperfect, and we all have a natural tendency toward fueling some drama. We should consider the nature and amount of the drama rather than striving for a completely drama-free environment. And when you are blessed to have a drama-free team, be thankful and do not take it for granted.

2. No one sees themselves as the one adding drama – it is always "others."

Over my years as a leader, I have never once heard someone say that they are contributing to office drama. But I have heard many tell me how OTHERS are. This is a common blind spot in teams – we fail to see how we are part of the problem, which is why feedback from others is so important.

3. Assess your team culture to see if unhealthy drama has taken root.

Diagnosing what is creating the drama cycle in an organization is not as easy as it may seem. Sometimes, an assessment or perspective from someone outside of the organization who is neutral and skilled can help the group to see itself more accurately.

4. Healthy staff can often counteract the impact of a drama king.

A number of years ago, an Australian researcher found that adding someone to a team who played the part of a jerk, downer, or slacker caused the overall performance of the team to drop dramatically. But not in every case. When the team had a skilled member or leader who could ask questions and control the situation in a healthy way, the team was impervious to the bad actor! So, don't underestimate how team members can have a positive impact on the drama queen, and be selective with who you hire.

5. Left unaddressed, drama can quickly become damaging and even deadly.

While most drama is annoying, at its worst, it can result in deadly outcomes. Some people can be extraordinarily sensitive to gossip or feel slighted to the point that they become depressed, anxious, or even dangerously angry. All it takes is one person with unbridled anger to result in a crisis. It is a leader's job to do his or her best to both monitor and manage the health of the team. And this is no easy task.

6. As a leader, ask yourself: "How may I be contributing to the drama?"

If it is hard for a team member to see how they may be a candidate for a drama king, it can be even harder for those who are in leadership. Being in charge does not make us immune to gossip, jealousy, or cliques. Perhaps it makes us even more vulnerable because we can more easily get away with it. The wise words of Jesus in Matthew 7 are worth heeding: look at yourself before looking at the behaviors of others.

7. Practice candor by addressing excessive or unhealthy drama rather than ignoring it.

Ignoring the wrong symptoms for too long can result in more serious issues later. In the context of unhealthy drama, this could include reduced morale, staff turnover, and decreased productivity. And quite often, it is the healthier members of the team who leave, resulting in an even worse environment.

10 Symptoms of a Team in Crisis

1. Increasing volume of undiscussed issues.
2. Lack of team chemistry and identity.
3. Deeply embedded perceptions of who is right/wrong.
4. Absence of joy, fun, and celebration.
5. Fragmented commitment to a shared vision and direction.
6. Relational pairing and triangulation.
7. Relational avoidance.
8. Pockets of eroded trust among team members.
9. Adaptation to a culture of dysfunction.
10. Spousal involvement in the conflict.

8 Ways to Facilitate Teamwork

1. Take time to build relationships with team members.
2. Emphasize your strengths and the strengths of others.
3. Avoid manipulation of other members.
4. Master interpersonal communication.
5. Walk in the shoes of other team members in order to build understanding.
6. Operate based on the team concept, even when it is not convenient.
7. Respect other members, even when you disagree.
8. Know yourself and other members as well as possible.

10 Steps to Delegation

1. Select people who are qualified or trained for the task.

2. Provide them with the necessary information and clear expectations.

3. Empower them with the necessary authority to accomplish the task.

4. Provide regular accountability and feedback.

5. Do not allow the task to be given back to you.

6. Provide encouragement to them along the way.

7. Don't expect the task to be done the way you would do it.

8. Expect success, but allow them the opportunity to fail.

9. Celebrate success with them.

10. Give public recognition of their success.

9 Reasons Why Leaders Fail to Delegate

1. They believe that no one can do the job as well as they can.

2. They don't want to invest the extra time to train others.

3. They fear losing influence and authority.

4. They are unwilling to give up recognition.

5. They are afraid to give up control.

6. They fear they won't be needed.

7. They are insecure that someone may do a better job than they did.

8. They experienced poor results when they previously delegated.

9. They are unaware of how to delegate.

✓ 6 Most Common Undiscussed Issues for Leaders

1. Why aren't we talking about "the less-than-stellar performance of this organization"? (Assessment)

2. Why aren't we talking about "why we are losing good people"? (Assessment)

3. Why aren't we talking about "possible distrust and conflict among us"? (Environment)

4. Why aren't we talking about "who will lead this organization in the event of sudden loss or retirement"? (Succession)

5. Why aren't we talking about "how to assess the effectiveness of the board and senior leader"? (Assessment)

6. Why aren't we talking about "our personal lives and feelings"? (Authenticity)

✅ 13 Steps for Hiring Staff

1. Assess the Organization

- Is the organization or team healthy enough to assimilate a new member?

- How ready is the hiring executive to commit the time required to make this process successful?

2. Build the Team

- Who will lead the hiring process?

- Do you have a labor attorney, human resource professional, or outside consulting group to help provide guidance?

- Do you have an environment of confidentiality?

3. Define the Position

- Why are you hiring for this position and not for another area in the organization?

- Are you filling current needs or future expectations?

- Does this position fit the strategic plan of the organization?

- If this is an existing position, what did the previous person do well/poorly?

4. Prepare the Job Description

- How would you summarize the position in 30 words or less?

- What 3-5 competencies are most critical for a person to succeed in this position?

- If you hired the right person for this position, what 3-5 outcomes would you expect to see in the next one, two, or three years?

- Does your job description include: title of the position; name or title of the person to whom the employee will report; educational requirements for this position; knowledge, skills, and abilities the employee will need to possess; supervisory responsibilities; primary qualifications and competencies; primary tasks/duties; expected outcomes and results; EOE/M/F/D/V compliant?

5. Determine Salary and Benefits Package

- Have you acquired both regional and national compensation data?

- How will this position fit the compensation guideline/policy adopted by the organization?

- What will the total compensation package (salary and benefits) consist of?

- How flexible are you with the starting salary? What is negotiable?

- Will there be future salary/benefit increases negotiated upfront, a signing bonus, or a relocation package?

6. Define the Parameters of the Search and Hiring Process

- Does your process reasonably align with the by-laws, as well as Federal and State laws?

- What are the time frame and recruitment budget?

- Will you retain a search firm?

7. Communicate Regularly

- What and how will you communicate with your organization, applicants, and lead candidates?

- How will those responsible for the search communicate with each other, the board or hiring executive, and the members at large?

8. Create an Application

- Do you have a thorough and legal application that has been reviewed by an attorney?

- Will a highly qualified candidate be willing to complete it?

- Will it include work history, education, references, or salary history?

9. Identify Applicants

- The six most common ways to identify applicants are through internal recruiting, internal postings, personal networking, external postings, a hiring coach, and a search firm. Which will you pursue and in what order?

10. Interview Applicants

- Utilize behavioral-based questions in the interview since past behavior is a solid indicator of future performance. Behavioral-based interviewing is the technique where the candidate is asked to talk about specific achievements or situations in his or her work career. Instead of asking, "Are you a strong leader?" say, "Describe a situation where you were a strong leader." Or simply ask for specific examples.

- When getting ready to interview a candidate, not only do you need to prepare the questions you will ask the applicant, but you will also need to be prepared for any questions they may ask you about the position and your organization.

11. Check References and Background

- Has your attorney created a Hold Harmless Release Form and do you have one signed by each candidate and reference?

- Are you planning to conduct additional background checks and do you have the appropriate signed releases for them?

- How will the reference checks be conducted (phone, face to face, written) and what questions will be asked?

- Are you planning to verify credentials? If so, how?

12. Assess Compatibility and Fit

- How are you planning to determine if a candidate is a good fit for your organization?

- Have you assessed if the candidate will be a fit with the culture, job description, leadership, supervisor(s) and team members, technical knowledge, skills, and abilities?

- Will you use assessment tests or surveys to assist you in determining fit?

13. Hire and Rejection

- Who will write the letter of hire and what will be included? Will they be offered a contract?

- Will the candidate be required to sign a Confidential Agreement or a Non-Compete Agreement? Has your legal counsel reviewed these agreements?

- What is a reasonable time frame to expect a candidate to respond?

- How will you communicate with those you are not planning to pursue?

Finding the Right "Fit" in Hiring

While competence, capacity, and character are important, compatibility, or "fit," is the most common cause of failure in hiring. Balance these elements when assessing a candidate.

CAPACITY
Fitness · Power ·
Room for more ·
Multi-tasking

COMPETENCY
Understanding ·
Acuity · Trustworthy ·
Inspires Change

FIT

CHARACTER
Integrity · Loyalty ·
Courage · Fortitude

COMPATIBILITY
Affinity · Accessibility ·
Complementing ·
Non-Competing

4 Mistakes in Hiring

1. The "Perfect Hire": This is an illusion, it does not exist.

2. Trust but not verify: Do your due diligence with background and references.

3. Close one eye: Overlook known deficits now, pay later.

4. Hire unilaterally: Wise people seek counsel. Confer with others before a hire.

10 Questions to Ask Before Firing Someone

1. How do you know you are accurate in your assessment? Is it documented?

2. Have you provided clear expectations and feedback?

3. Will the staff member be surprised by the transition?

4. Have you considered if you played any role in his or her lack of success?

5. Do you have a communication plan and timeline for the transition?

6. Have you sought a legal review of your rationale, plan, and separation agreement?

7. Is your public message honest, wise, and agreed upon by the staff member?

8. Do you know how you will fill the gap left in the wake of the transition?

9. What, if any, severance will be provided?

10. Have you written a separation agreement? What should it include?

10 Reminders When Sharing Difficult Decisions

1. **Credibility:** Use your most credible and capable leaders to speak publicly.

2. **Transparency:** Strive towards as much disclosure as appropriate.

3. **Humility:** Manifest a humble spirit both publicly and privately.

4. **Self-control:** Don't be drawn into a debate or manifest an argumentative spirit.

5. **Hope:** Regularly share hope and vision for the future of the organization.

6. **Consistency:** Be sure your messages and rationale remain consistent.

7. **Awareness:** Monitor the internet and social media for positive or negative communication.

8. **Courage:** Don't allow fear of man to govern your decision.

9. **Unity:** Work diligently to guard the unity of the board/staff.

10. **Caution:** Guard your own hearts, spirits, and families against some of the negative short-term effects that arise during significant change.

26 Common Errors in Leadership Transition

The leadership transition process creates both exciting opportunity but also vulnerability. Mistakes are inevitable during a leadership search. Here are 26 common errors we have seen organizations make during the transition process. We desire to help leaders guard against these errors and thereby increase the likelihood of a successful leadership change.

1. Assuming you don't have any "hairline cracks" or serious problems to address within the organization.

2. Providing inadequate and infrequent communication to the organization.

3. Allowing the organization to go on a holding pattern during the transition process.

4. Ignoring significant undiscussed issues among the remaining leadership.

5. Having conflict and trust issues within the staff, leadership, or overall organization, but still moving forward with the search.

6. Launching a search process prematurely.

7. Failing to utilize, pay attention to, communicate with, and care for the remaining staff whose knowledge may be helpful and whose anxiety may be heightened.

8. Avoiding succession discussion and planning due to fear of conflict with the existing staff member or leader.

9. Allowing the transitioning staff member to have too much influence in the search and hiring process.

10. Allowing a previous leader to stay on staff in a different role without carefully considering the risks with the new leader.

11. Failing to "finish well" with the existing staff member including agreed-upon expectations of behavior.

12. Assuming you can conduct a search the way you did the last time, which may have been 20-30 years ago.

13. Failing to develop a clear, compelling, and unifying sense of vision and priorities before making the new hire.

14. Failing to develop an agreed-upon profile for the next successful candidate.

15. Creating cumbersome steps in the process such as a lengthy application.

16. Using an interim leader who has aspirations to be the next leader.

17. Using an interim or temp person to fill a position without clearly managing expectations.

18. Failing to acquire legal counsel at critical points in the transition and hiring process.

19. Having inadequate skills and experience within the leadership or staff to conduct a successful recruitment process.

20. Developing "search fatigue" that results in prematurely hiring a candidate who may not be the best choice.

21. Looking for a candidate who is an "A" in every category including leader, manager, relater, and visionary.

22. Underestimating the importance of a candidate's spouse (if married) in senior-level leadership positions.

23. Failing to conduct adequate background and reference checks.

24. Failing to adequately assess the candidate for fit with the organization, leadership, and staff.

25. Spiritualizing your decisions by claiming, "This is God's person for us."

26. Failing to realize a mistake in the hiring process will cost you a lot of money and pain, often reaching $150,000-$250,000.

People don't resist change; they resist being changed.

– Peter Senge

7 Culture Builders to Attract & Retain Your Best People

1. Incorporate appropriate humor and celebration into your environment.

When you step into an attractive culture, you can feel and hear the difference. You commonly hear laughter, see smiles, and discover shared meals and celebrations for special accomplishments.

2. Care for one another by meeting needs and showing interest.

This can be as simple as asking someone about their weekend or as significant as mobilizing the team to help a sick member by providing meals, gift cards, or picking up their workload. A caring culture is a sticky culture – one that people will be slow to leave.

3. Model competency in your work by being the best at what you do.

No one wants to work with a dud. A positive culture also requires talent – people showing up for work, working hard, knowing how to do their job, and doing it with excellence. Tolerating an incompetent team member will have a cascading negative effect on the other members as well as the overall reputation and culture of the organization.

4. Express positivity both verbally and in how you present yourself.

When one researcher planted an actor into different teams with the job of acting like a downer, jerk, or slacker, the performance of most of the teams declined by 30-40%!

Eeyore from Winnie the Pooh would not make for a good recruitment poster.

5. Provide opportunities for growth and advancement.

A good culture is one where people have the chance to grow, learn, and advance. With a little creativity, this can be done even in the smallest organizations. Challenging assignments, financial incentives, and educational opportunities are just a few ways to build your culture through growth opportunities.

6. Include others by asking for their input and feedback.

The COVID-19 pandemic resulted in an extended season of separation. A recent survey by global commercial real estate services company JLL found that 70% of office workers felt being in the workplace was more helpful for collaborating, solving complex issues, and connecting with leadership[1]. All of these involve communication and feedback which make people feel included.

7. Hire for cultural fit, not just skill.

In the typical job description, you will likely find a detailed list of technical competencies with a few generic phrases regarding being a "people person" or "getting along well with others." Yet, it is poor cultural fit that most often results in the failure of team members. There is no infallible way to assess for cultural fit, but knowing what you value and including your best people in the hiring process can help.

---

1   "Global workforce expectations are shifting due to COVID-19," *JLL Research*, 17 November 2020, jll.de.

✅ 20 Characteristics of Effective Team Leaders

1. Their dreams are greater than their memories.

2. They know when and how to ask for help (seek counsel).

3. They learn from multiple sources outside of their field.

4. They understand the importance of emotional intelligence.

5. They leverage their culture (it is not the enemy of their success).

6. They know how to let their "gut" (intuition) and their brain work synergistically.

7. They build a team culture not necessarily a family culture.

8. They are constantly refining their focus until it is laser-like.

9. They live their values authentically (and talk about them frequently).

10. Their generosity is normal, not rare.

11. They are approachable even when the news is bad.

12. They trust the trustworthy with high-level tasks.

13. They truly enjoy their team. They know how to have fun.

14. They monitor and manage morale.

15. They don't use excuses to justify the loss of momentum.

16. They are constantly engaging, not withdrawing.

17. They love and seek truth. The proof is they stay humble.

18. They resolve problems quickly.

19. They look for opportunities to praise, honor, and recognize excellence in others.

20. Others respect them because they practice the first 19 characteristics.

Do not wait to strike till the iron is hot;
make it hot by striking.

WILLIAM SPRAGUE

CHAPTER EIGHT

Personal Growth & Development

7 Signs of the Self-Destructing Leader: Are You One?

As leaders, none of us are immune to behaviors and thoughts that can ultimately lead to self-destruction. We have watched many leaders, including pastors, head slowly but surely towards a crash, taking their organization along with them. And the scariest part is they do not even know it's happening. Here are the signs of a self-destructing leader. In most cases, more than one sign is present before the crash takes place. Do you see any of these signs in your life?

1. Pride

We often hear Proverbs 16:18 quoted: "Pride comes before destruction." Jim Collins's book on *How the Mighty Fall* and Dr. Mortimer Feinberg's writing on *Why Smart People Do Dumb Things* both remind us that a self-destructing leader is often standing on a foundation of pride, and this pride contributes to all of the following signs of self-destruction. I recall a time when a board member wanted to hire us to help an organization plan for succession, but the top leader put the brakes on it. Why? Because he believed he knew better than everyone else!

2. Fear of feedback

Self-destructing leaders avoid feedback at all costs. Suggest a 360° feedback assessment, and they will find 101 reasons why not to do it. They fear that what they hear may shatter the image they hold of themselves and may weaken their control of the organization. I remember one leader who, after completing a 360° feedback assessment, expressed serious anger. He could not accept that his team members were providing him with valuable critique, and he would not listen to their input. And, he eventually destructed.

3. Taking credit for success

Self-destructing leaders love to take credit for all of the success. Why? Because it reinforces the broken view they hold of themselves: they are the cause of all of the success that their organization has experienced. And, they believe if someone else is contributing to this success, it may weaken their position and control and people may start to value others more than them!

4. Blaming others for mistakes

"It's always someone else's fault." That is the motto of the self-destructing leader. They have an image to maintain and, even though it is one built on self-deception, the self-destructing leader works hard to keep it going. This is often done by blaming others for anything that goes wrong.

5. Punishing those who disagree

Like a dictator in an authoritarian regime, self-destructing leaders have a habit of punishing and banishing those who challenge them. This can include marginalizing, demonizing, or even firing. The result is pretty much the same – people learn to not tell the king that he is naked! Many employees have told me that they don't want to share their thoughts with a leader because they have seen too many people punished for doing so.

6. Isolation

This is what psychologists refer to as social-distance (not in the context of health) – keeping the majority of people far enough away from your personal life and thoughts in order to maintain the illusion of success. After a leader has destructed, we often hear statements from clients like, "She was a private person," or "We have never been to his home." Such leaders compartmentalize their lives, separating public from private with very high firewalls. The self-destructing leader is a lot like the Wizard in the Wizard of Oz, just a little flawed human hidden behind a curtain using a lot of special effects!

7. Mental health issues

According to the Substance Abuse and Mental Health Services Administration, there are over 52 million Americans living with some form of mental health illness[1]. I know many leaders who struggle with anxiety or depression and have gotten the professional help needed to manage it. However, there are leaders who have either an undiagnosed or unmanaged mental health issue which can result in destructive choices.

As leaders, every one of us has likely struggled with one or more of these signs. The difference is that a self-destructive leader manifests multiple signs which have become a pattern of his or her behavior. As a consultant, I have seen self-destructive behavior showing up especially in leaders who are in their mid-fifties and early sixties. Some of them have led well for many years but are now showing cracks in how they think and lead, with sad results. If you are a self-destructing leader or you either supervise one or work with one, an experienced coach can provide the guidance you need to bring about healthy change.

---

1   "Key Substance Use and Mental Health Indicators in the United States: Results from the 2020 National Survey on Drug Use and Health," *Substance Abuse and Mental Health Services Administration*, 2021.

 7 Signs That You Really Are a Leader

People are infatuated with the concept of leadership. We have seen this many times over the years of teaching, consulting, and coaching with people expressing their desire to get promoted and become senior-level players in their organizations. But, how do you know if you are truly leading? Here are seven signs that you really are a leader.

1. Your team chooses to follow you rather than feels forced to follow you.

If you see someone claiming to be a leader but using bullying or threats to get people to follow them – they are anything but a leader. Why? Because leaders depend on influence for gathering followers rather than coercion. Leaders depend on relationship, competence, and trust, not manipulation, threat, and title. Every leader should be humble and teachable enough to discover, "Is my team following me by choice or by coercion?"

2. You are having a few sleepless nights.

Leadership is stressful. Not all the time, but often. There are hard decisions to make. Personnel to manage. Changes to implement. These are the elements of leadership, and there are no guarantees your decisions will prove to be correct. Because of this, most leaders do experience some hard nights. So, if you have some sleepless nights due to the weight of a leadership decision, that is not only normal, but it is also a reminder that leaders carry burdens on behalf of their organizations.

3. You are feeling some fears, insecurities, or doubts.

If a leader acts excessively confident all the time, either he is faking it or he is a bit abnormal. Leaders are often faced with situations that can and sometimes do go off the rails with just one misstatement or misstep. This can surface doubts regarding your competency, and elevate fears of losing your job, being demonized, or perhaps being sued. So, if you have no fear and doubt, you may have more to fear than you know.

4. You are taking some risks that have no guarantees of success.

Related to #2 and #3, a leader who takes no risks is not worthy of the position. I was recently talking to a friend who runs a large organization. He spent a truckload of money on preparations to open his organization during the pandemic. It was a big risk. If things go bad, he could lose a significant amount of money. But the vision of most organizations requires taking risks, and leaders know there are no guarantees of success.

5. You are hearing some criticism about yourself or your organization.

Compliments feel good, right? We all love to be affirmed and told how valuable and important we are. But criticism? That doesn't feel good to most people. Jesus warned against the dangers of when everyone speaks well of you. Why? Because a leader is often in a position that will result in some people despising him or her. A friend of mine once said, "Leadership can feel like being pecked to death by ducks!" So, if you have no peck marks, you are either in a nice lull or you may not be leading much.

6. You do not ask your team to do anything you are unwilling to do.

A few years ago, while preparing for a conference, I heard a young team member make an observant comment about his boss: "Everyone is helping to set up chairs except him!" While there could have been a legitimate explanation for why the boss was not helping, it does elevate the importance of leading by serving and that real leaders are willing to get dirty themselves. In other words, rather than just being "tellers," they are "modelers."

7. You are often and genuinely affirmed by others for your leadership.

When a person models positive leadership strengths, people take notice. Especially other talented leaders. When I was young, one of the people I looked up to as a leader and mentor often affirmed my leadership skills and potential. He did this through notes, by sharing it over a meal, and by creating new leadership opportunities that would stretch me. His affirmation served as a confidence builder and growth enhancer. So, pay attention to what you are hearing from others.

5 Errors of Goal Setting

A goal is a desired outcome toward which you direct intentional energy and resources to achieve. A goal is a specific, measurable accomplishment to be achieved within a specific time frame.

1. Goal Confusion

Goal confusion comes from ambiguity. Be clear, concise, and consistent in the use of terms such as mission, vision, values, strategy, key objective, priority, tactic, outcome, action step, long-term or short-term goal, etc. Confusing right?

2. "Wishful" Goals

Having specific metrics with methods to achieve them works much better than a "magic wand" or "three wishes."

3. Unplanned Goals

There is no shortage of new opportunities or nagging obstacles. Without focus, these things will pull the leader off course, and the obstacles and opportunities become the new goals.

4. Unrealistic Goals

Unrealistic goals happen when we create too many goals or are too aggressive in our expectations of the goals we have. Verify the time, leadership bandwidth, and resources that are needed to be successful, and attempt no more than 3-5 goals at the same time.

5. Forgotten Goals

Forgotten goals happen when we are content to create a document and "leave it on a shelf." They happen when we are pleased with activity over results and the urgent over the important. Keep your goals visible and celebrate mile markers.

7 Principles Regarding Time Management

1. Everyone has limited time and unlimited opportunities. Therefore, the ultimate way to manage time is to make wise decisions.

2. Your calendar follows your values. Focus on managing your priorities, and it will be easier to manage your calendar.

3. People will sometimes applaud unhealthy behavior. If you have a high need to be accepted, your calendar will be controlled by others rather than you.

4. Be cautious in using others as the standard by which you measure yourself. We all have different energy levels and capacities.

5. The most important things in life are usually not urgent. Therefore, if you always invest your time in the urgent, the important will usually be neglected.

6. Prune your calendar in order to create enough margin for when the unexpected happens.

7. Reflect upon your long-term life goals. What do you want to be able to say about your use of time when your life nears its end?

"Until we can manage time, we can manage nothing else."

— Peter F. Drucker

8 Ways to Prevent Burnout

1. Know yourself and your limits.

2. Stay focused on your priorities.

3. Practice saying "no" to someone or something.

4. Reduce the number of decisions/choices.

5. Spend time with people you enjoy.

6. Limit long-term commitments.

7. Find a way to exercise that is a fit for you.

8. Delegate! Mobilize others to share the load and the credit.

6 Steps to Prepare for an Interview

1. Do your research.

What does the organization say about itself? Check their website for their history, core values, mission, vision, reputation in the community, background and experience of their key leaders, and the local demographics.

2. Anticipate the questions you will likely be asked.

Be prepared to answer each of those questions briefly, but let the interviewer know you would be happy to elaborate if they desire. It is usually helpful if you can give specific illustrations of experiences you have had that are germane to the question. Certainly be prepared to describe accurately why you have left or are willing to leave your current place of employment, if applicable. Employers will often want to know about your specific skill sets, personal life ambitions, etc. It may be helpful to be prepared to share lessons you have learned through your failures as well as your successes.

3. Watch for a "right fit" in the organization.

If you can't be honest and authentic, you will have a difficult time identifying and communicating if you are truly compatible with the organization. It is important that you have a sense of the type of environment where you will thrive and make a valid contribution. All employment opportunities are not right for you as a uniquely gifted individual.

4. Understand the whole process.

Be sure to clarify what the whole process looks like so you can adjust your expectations appropriately. If there are multiple interviews in the process, this may affect when you will get various pieces of information from the organization (compensation, expectations, specific job requirements, etc.). The timing of the questions you desire to ask will also be affected by the process.

5. Know what you want to know.

Have a list of specific things you want to learn formally and informally about this organization. Formulate your questions and look for the best (most appropriate) time to ask them.

6. Know and avoid the areas that cannot legally be addressed.

Federal law defines some areas of life that cannot be probed during an interview.

20 Traits of Those Who Get Hired

Most organizations are looking for a combination of the following skills or traits when they make a hire:

1. **Charisma:** Do you have the ability to inspire others?

2. **Courage:** Do you stand up for what you believe even if it causes hardship?

3. **Dependability:** Do you faithfully accept and keep responsibilities, always following through?

4. **Effective Communicator:** Is your speech and writing concise, accurate, and compelling?

5. **Flexibility:** Do you function effectively in changing environments?

6. **Fostering Teamwork and Diversity:** Do you tend to create a collaborative effort where everyone feels valued?

7. **Genuine Concern and Respect for Others:** Is serving others part of your motivational behavior? Do you honor them and not belittle them regardless of their position?

8. **Getting Results:** Can you implement strategies and tactics that fulfill the mission/vision?

9. **Global Mindset:** Are you a BIG picture person rather than myopic?

10. **Integrative Thinker:** Are you able to blend accurately many viewpoints, datasets, and factors?

11. **Integrity:** Are you a person known for good character, who does what is ethical and moral and does not abuse freedoms?

12. **Intellectual Stimulation:** Are you able to help others problem solve?

13. **Intelligent Risk Taking:** What decision-making criteria do you use when innovating or leading?

14. **Judgment:** Have you proven yourself to be discerning, objective, rational, and logical?

15. **Making People Better:** Are others strengthened and encouraged by working with you?

16. **Unique Competencies:** Are you an expert at anything?

17. **Personal Involvement:** Do you show interest in others through active listening and offering to coach them?

18. **Self-Awareness:** Have you made personal changes based on seeking and receiving honest feedback?

19. **Technical Excellence:** What elements of the digital world have you mastered?

20. **Thinking Like a Leader:** Can you direct people and resources towards accomplishing goals?

"In the absence of clearly defined goals, we become strangely loyal to daily acts of trivia."

— *Unknown*

4 Questions That Will Make a Difference in Choosing Your Next Job

Whether you are 22 or 52, there is a very good chance that you will experience a time when you are trying to figure out "what next?" Over the years, I have talked with many different men and women, both younger and older, as they wrestle with decisions regarding whether to stay at a job, to leave, or which out of two or three options may be best. For some, it is exciting! But for others, it can be a confusing and anxiety-producing time, especially if they make a mistake. Here are four questions that can help you as you think about both your present position as well as your possible next job. While each person may weigh these differently, our experience has demonstrated that ignoring any one of them will likely result in future dissatisfaction.

RELATIONSHIPS

Who will I be working for and with, and how much will I enjoy these relationships?

JOB

Will the nature of the job fit with my strengths, passion, and personality?

LOCATION

Will the location be a good fit relating to my needs? (medical, temperature, schools, aging parents...)

COMPENSATION

How much will I be paid, will the needs of my family be met, and will I be satisfied?

CHAPTER NINE

Planning & Organizing

Time is a precious gift – every second, every minute, every day – use it wisely. You cannot pay the cost of losing time.

SONNY GANN

8 Things to Know Before Developing a Strategic Plan

1. Know what problems you are trying to "solve" (present or future).

2. Know the current realities of your organization (honest assessment needed).

3. Know who is a part of the planning and why. "Get the right people on the bus." – Jim Collins

4. Know if you are looking for voice from others or just a "rubber stamp."

5. Know plans often fail because they are too complex (keep it simple).

6. Know the process you are following (consider a facilitator).

7. Know there is no such thing as "painless change."

8. Know that the success of the plan will be directly related to the resources available and the desire and capability of the people involved.

3 Phases of Strategic Planning

Strategic planning determines where an organization is going and how it is going to get there. Creating a plan clarifies the purpose of the organization as well as provides leaders and participants with a shared vision of the "big picture" that includes the role of individuals and their tasks within it. An effective plan provides a greater opportunity to coordinate specific operations and delegate responsibility.

1. Listening: Assessment Phase

- Create voice within your organization.

- Seek a clear and honest picture of the organization at present. Look at the various Strengths, Weaknesses, Opportunities, and Threats regarding the organization (SWOT).

- Discern the stated, unstated, and perceived values of the organization from leaders, regular participants, and casual observers.

- What values are currently being expressed by your budget, staffing, energies, etc. "Show me your calendar and show me your checkbook, and I will tell you what you really believe."

- Explore the organization's unique DNA. What is inherent to your organization by nature of your founding, the hearts of your leaders, and the circumstances of your history?

2. Learning: Alignment Phase

- Collecting data is easy, but interpreting that data is hard. The goal of learning is to be able to use the information gathered to properly align the major elements of the organization such as goals, budgets, staffing, programming, and facilities.

- Decide what things you need to STOP doing in order to make the right adjustments to align the mission and vision.

- Create a 36-month game plan (a Priority-Based Action Plan) complete with strategies, tactics, metrics, and mile-markers to monitor progress.

- Clarify lines of authority and decision-making, especially in new areas.

3. Leading: Action Phase

- Determine specific assignments, for specific people, on specific timetables which will provide opportunities to evaluate, recognize, and celebrate progress.

- Provide early and ongoing communication to those implementing the plan and those impacted by it. Group meetings often provide appropriate accountability and encouragement.

- Encourage celebration. Reward high-performing teams and individuals (you get what you honor: i.e. whatever you affirm, you get more of the same).

- Stay agile. Resist the temptation to lose focus by chasing new opportunities or becoming preoccupied with solving endless problems. Navigating the organization to the identified destination means "keeping a steady hand on the rudder" when you feel tossed up and down by obstacles and opportunities. This requires constantly adapting and adopting.

Adapting: Solving problems and removing obstacles

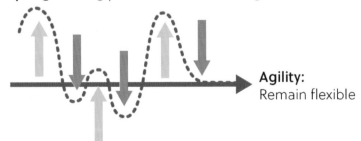

Agility: Remain flexible

Adopting: Exploiting new opportunities

A SWOT Analysis with a Twist

Consider a group discussion around these quadrants to expose the areas to be addressed in a strategic planning process.

ADVANTAGES What we do better than most others in our field **DO ACCENTUATE**	**ADVANCEMENTS** Innovations, technologies, or environments that will likely benefit us **DO ADOPT**
IMPROVEMENTS Areas that need our attention to maximize our effectiveness **DO ADDRESS**	**DANGERS** Likely obstacles that we will need to navigate to remain an industry leader **DO ADAPT**

7 Reasons Why Plans Fail

1. Leading without listening.

2. Starting with the future instead of the past.

3. Asking the wrong questions.

4. Complexity rather than simplicity.

5. Objectives without champions.

6. Destinations without demarcation (metrics).

7. The illusion of pain-free planning.

5 Steps to Identifying Organizational Gaps

Step 1

List all regularly scheduled activities and programs of your organization (anything that takes time, money, facilities, or staff to accomplish).

Step 2

Assign a priority level of 1-4 to every program.

- **Level 1 Priority – ESSENTIAL:** Absolutely integral to your mission, vision, and core values.

- **Level 2 Priority – IMPORTANT:** Important for health, growth, and momentum, but NOT absolute essentials.

- **Level 3 Priority – ENJOYED:** Non-essential but still valued and enjoyed by the membership.

- **Level 4 Priority – TOLERATED:** Often labeled as "sacred cows." Their usefulness to the organization is limited and they are now viewed by most as a hindrance rather than a help. For political or economic reasons, these activities remain.

Step 3

Assign a resource draw factor to each program (resources include human, financial, time, space, etc.). H = high draw, M = moderate draw, and L = low draw.

Step 4

Assign an effectiveness grade to each area (A-E).

A. Great, performing as intended. No improvement is needed.

B. Good value to the organization. Small, non-urgent improvements needed.

C. Average at best. Improvements needed sooner rather than later.

D. Poor outcomes, complete overhaul needed.

E. Detrimental, hurting momentum and stealing resources.

Step 5
Take Action. I = Improve it, C = Cut it, or M = Maintain it.

PROGRAM ALIGNMENT GAP ANALYSIS

List All Programs	Priority Level (1,2,3,4)	Resource Draw (H,M,L)	Effectiveness Grade (A,B,C,D,F)	Alignment Action (I,C,M)

5 Focusing Questions That Lead to Action

Planning will be incomplete if the leader cannot clearly communicate the answers to these five questions that keep the planning process coordinated and focused.

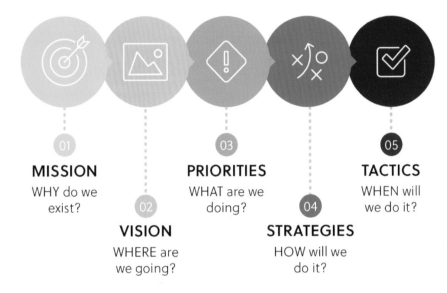

01

MISSION

WHY do we exist?

02

VISION

WHERE are we going?

03

PRIORITIES

WHAT are we doing?

04

STRATEGIES

HOW will we do it?

05

TACTICS

WHEN will we do it?

7 Ways to Listen

1. Intentionally creating feedback opportunities in each meeting.

2. Confidential interviews done by a third party.

3. Focus groups.

4. Whole-system surveys.

5. Walk-around management (casual and personal connection).

6. "After Action Reports" following events.

7. Suggestion box (recognize and reward valuable contributions).

8 Tests for Your Organizational Structure

1. Are we making strategic decisions in a timely manner?

2. Are we seeing tactical implementation take place in a timely manner?

3. Is our staff balanced between tactical leaders and visionary leaders?

4. Is our structure flexible enough to adapt to new environments?

5. Is there any significant role confusion between staff members or the staff and board?

6. Does our structure provide protection of the organization by way of staff accountability?

7. Is there regular communication that keeps key stakeholders in the loop regarding planning and changes?

8. Are we experiencing a sense of joy in our work environment?

4 Ways to Manage Information

1. **File it:** Create a file system and place important papers in the appropriate files.

2. **Act on it:** Respond immediately to emails, texts, and phone messages that only require a simple answer.

3. **Transfer it:** Send the note or message to the appropriate person, and ask the person to ensure closure.

4. **Trash it:** Get rid of it. With technological resources, if you need it later, it will be easy enough to find.

✅ 6 Great Time Wasters at Work

1. Casual Conversation

Casual conversation is actually an important part of healthy relationships and showing concern for others. However, when not managed appropriately, it can eat away at your time and the time of those with whom you talk.

2. Internet

The internet has become an essential part of our work lives. We do research, keep up with important news, and learn about services and people that matter to our work. Yet, it can also easily drift into meaningless surfing and game playing that squanders hours each week.

3. Social Media

While there are many benefits to social media, inappropriate or excessive use at work can waste a lot of important time and also rob your employer.

4. E-mail

E-mail is our best friend and worst enemy. It makes us readily accessible and yet easily overwhelms our capacity to prioritize, sort, and respond. Email must be used wisely and managed appropriately, or it may drain your time tank.

5. Meetings

In a knowledge-based and experience-based world, meetings are not only important, but they are also essential for maintaining trust, sharing ideas, sharing ownership, and collaborating on new initiatives and solutions. However, meetings can also suck the life out of us if not purposeful and enjoyable.

6. Personal life

We often spend 45-55 hours per week at work. Our personal lives need not stop when we enter the office. Those who we work with can provide encouragement, a sounding board, and a nice diversion from other life stresses. However, personal conversation needs to be both self-monitored and managed or it will eat away both others' and your time.

5 Ways to Manage Your Time

1. Consider the level of importance of the activities in which you are investing your time.

2. Look at the urgency of the activities in which you are investing your time including social media.

3. Organize your goals based on important things rather than urgent things.

4. Capitalize on the strengths of others by not doing what someone else can do.

5. Keep asking the question, "Does this need to be done now or at all?"

Focus: Leverage Concentrated Effort for Maximum Performance

1. Find something you love doing.

2. Define your VIPs (very important priorities).

3. Limit your daily diet of information.

4. Reduce activity addiction.

5. Guard against inattentional blindness (missing what is right in front of you).

Straightforward Succession Planning

The leader who is transitioning and the senior leadership/board need to have candid conversations about the following categories to avoid misunderstandings, conflict, and transitions that are injurious to the organization. Select one variable in each category to begin forming the right transitional plan. Who has the authority to decide each variable will depend on the nature of the organization.

Note: Your specific context will determine the pros, cons, and nuances of each variable.

Pick a Purpose (Why)
- Transition to another type of work
- Full retirement
- Semi-retirement
- Illness
- Other:

Pick a Time Frame (When)
- Immediately
- 6 months – 1 year
- 1 year – 2 years
- 3 years – 5 years
- Other:

Pick a Package (How Much)
- Nothing
- One-time financial payment
- 3-6 months + benefits

- 6-9 months + benefits
- 9-12 months + benefits
- Insurance coverage for _____ months
- Other:

Pick a Model

- Relay race (leader stays and passes the baton before leaving)
- Promote from within (already in the system)
- "New sheriff in town" (search outside the system)
- Consider a different leadership model
- Other:

Pick a Transition Sequence (More than one may apply)

- Change the model before the transition
- Hire the successor before the transition
- Hire the successor after the transition
- Hire and exchange roles slowly (mentee to co-leader to leader)
- Other:

Pick a Search Scope

- Internal candidate
- External regional
- External national
- External international
- Other:

Pick a Search Process

- Internal search team (usually described in the bylaws)
- Hire a company to provide applicants
- Hybrid (hire a search assistance firm)
- Other:

Pick a Communication Strategy

- Announce changes now, amend bylaws, make changes
- Announce now, start the process of transition
- Announce 6 months from transition
- Announce 1 year from transition
- Announce 18 months from transition
- Other:

Pick a Posture (Advice to the transitioning Leader)

- Stay full-time as a consultant or in a new role
- Stay and be part-time as a consultant or in a new role
- Stay in the area and serve as a volunteer
- Leave but plan to come back for special events
- Move on and don't come around for a while (1 year etc.)
- Take another position with another organization
- Other:

Setting Policy

Use a guide to create consistency in the formation of policies. Policies should always be written and include the following:

- Policy Name:

- Policy Number:

- Approved By:

- Approval Date:

- Effective Date:

- Expiration Date:
  Usually 3-5 years

- Review Date:
  Review, revise as needed, and renew the policy

- Historical Context for this Policy:
  Why was this policy needed at this time?

- Rationale for the Policy:
  What is this policy attempting to prevent or cause?

- Application:
  To whom does this policy apply?

- Distribution/Communication Plan:
  Who needs to be informed?

- Actual Policy Wording:
  Be clear, be concise, be consistent.

Effective leadership is not about making speeches or being liked; leadership is defined by results not attributes.

PETER DRUCKER

CHAPTER TEN

Leadership

How to Know You Are NOT a Narcissistic Leader

What is a narcissist? The simple answer: you know when you meet one or work for one! According to psychologists Alan Cavaiola and Neil Lavender, after being around a narcissist, you will often feel demeaned, inadequate, unappreciated, and angry. Narcissism is when a person has an extraordinarily high view of oneself and falls far short of empathy towards others. Psychologists have tested a number of college students over the past 30 years and have noted a continuous increase in narcissism during this time.[1] So, here are seven ways to know you are not a narcissistic leader.

1. If you are known more for building others up than tearing others down – you are less likely to be a narcissist.

2. If you understand and acknowledge your flaws and limitations rather than exaggerate your strengths and value to the organization – you are less likely to be a narcissist.

3. If you give credit to others rather than take it all yourself – you are less likely to be a narcissist.

4. If you name drop to add value to a conversation rather than to look good – you are less likely to be a narcissist.

5. If you invest in others rather than take advantage of them for your own benefit – you are less likely to be a narcissist.

---

[1] Twenge, J. M., & Foster, J. D. "Birth Cohort Increases in Narcissistic Personality Traits Among American College Students, 1982-2009," *Social Psychological and Personality Science*, 2010.

6. If you both feel empathy and show empathy towards others – you are less likely to be a narcissist.

7. If you look out for the interest of others rather than acting as though you are entitled to more than others – you are less likely to be a narcissist.

Seldom do any of us leaders know how we are doing in these seven areas without feedback from truthful colleagues, friends, and coaches. We would all do well to remember the wise words from Ann Landers, "Don't accept your dog's admiration as conclusive evidence that you are wonderful."

5 Questions Leaders Should Regularly Ask Their Team

Questions enhance communication, show interest, and improve learning. Here are five questions leaders would be smart to start regularly asking their team in order to improve culture.

1. How are you? (your spouse, children, weekend plans, challenges)

2. Is there anything I can do to help you? (stress, projects, resources, expectations)

3. How are you feeling about…? (life, work, position, the organization)

4. What am I doing right? (coaching, encouraging, rewarding, providing opportunities)

5. What can I do better? (expectations, encouragement, time, give credit)

Top 6 Actions for Board Effectiveness in the Coming Decade

1. Get smaller
It is increasingly difficult to find board members with the talent and time to serve well, and a large board can be unwieldy in both scheduling and group dynamics.

2. Get better
Boards may find greater benefit from a smaller group of highly talented members versus a larger group that is a mix of exceptional members and average ones.

3. Get purposeful
Meetings should be compelling - focused on higher-level policy and strategic tasks rather than lower-level operational tasks.

4. Get agreement
Every member understands expectations including the type of board, scope of authority, rules of behavior, character, and fundraising. You must know which hat you are wearing!

5. Get flexible
Effective boards are nimble. Adjust board membership, frequency of meetings, and agenda topics based on the quickly changing needs of the organization and the external environment.

6. Get sustainable
This consists of a compelling vision, credible leadership, wisely planned succession, and long-term financial funding.

10 Tips for Managing a Crisis

Unexpected things happen. An employee embezzles funds. A disgruntled staff member attacks another member. A volunteer sexually assaults a constituent. Such crises can threaten the operations, reputation, and overall health and well-being of the organization. While the crisis itself is damaging enough, it can get worse when managed unwisely. Here are 10 tips for managing an organizational crisis.

1. Act!

Be quick and decisive. Ignoring what is emerging or delaying taking action will only allow the situation to worsen. If the crisis poses a threat to public safety, the primary concern should be to act quickly to ensure the safety of others. Failure to do so will increase the damage from the crisis.

2. Learn.

Don't jump to conclusions prematurely. Gather the facts before making statements and major decisions. Premature decisions or incomplete information can result in making the crisis worse.

3. Seek Guidance.

It is often valuable to seek legal, organizational, and public relations counsel early on when managing a crisis. Your insurance company will often provide counsel as well.

4. Inform.

Depending on the nature of your organization and the crisis, it is wise to inform those above you regarding what is taking place. This may be a supervisor, board, insurance carrier, or legal authority.

5. Be visible.
Demonstrate that someone is in charge and working to make things better. A visible leader will calm the natural uncertainty and anxiety that arise during such critical events.

6. Put people first.
In a crisis, leaders will sometimes adopt a "cover yourself/the organization" attitude. Don't allow utilitarianism to prevail by placing personal or organizational interests first. Put people first. Depending upon the circumstances, it may be those who believe they were harmed or those who were accused.

7. Own it.
If there is something the leader or organization needs to take responsibility for, do it. Apologizing is always the right thing to do even if the crisis was unintentional. However, some apology strategies are much more effective than others. If you desire to put those affected by the crisis first, take note of the following four practices when apologizing.

- Don't attack the accuser.
- Don't blame others for the crisis.
- Don't deny that the crisis happened.
- Don't make excuses for why the crisis happened.

Taking responsibility and offering a sincere apology go a long way in healing.

8. Communicate liberally and consistently.

Designate a primary communicator. For the sake of clarity and to maintain consistency, one person should represent the leadership in all matters of public or official comment. Additionally, the best way to prevent or minimize rumors is to share as many of the facts as possible. Make sure what you share is accurate and consistent. When mistakes are made, they must be corrected, but that will also make the organization look incompetent. Be honest about what you know and what you do not know, and do not speculate.

9. Document everything.

Keep a file of notes and documentation to help you acquire a clear understanding and make wise decisions. Such a file should be kept in a secure place since it will contain very confidential information.

10. Declare an end.

Some organizations perpetuate a crisis by continuing to make it the focal point for too long of a period of time. Remember, the crisis is not the mission. It is important to officially declare an end to the crisis (but not prematurely) and once again share the compelling vision for the future.

6 Reminders for Leading Effectively During a Crisis

We all face uncertainties as we navigate leadership in the "uncharted waters" of our world today. None of us know with absolute certainty how it will all turn out. But for many of us, we know the mission has not changed. The way we accomplish our mission may look very different in the future than it has in the past. Here are six strategies to help leaders navigate a crisis while keeping their organization focused on its mission.

1. Don't lose focus.

It is easy to be distracted and pulled off course. In a crisis, there can be many voices trying to tell you what you should be doing. Remember your mission.

2. Don't be afraid to lead.

Communicate and provide direction. Your voice should have a ring of clarity, calmness, and confidence. If you have been put in a leadership role, you are there for times such as these.

3. Trust your crew.

Hopefully, you have people that are capable and skilled. Give expanded responsibility and authority to act to those in whom you have great trust. You will never be able to do it alone, nor should you try.

4. Seek wise counsel.

Proverbs 15 reminds us that wise people seek wise counsel. A sense of invulnerability or self-sufficiency is just another manifestation of one's arrogance and enlarged ego. Pride comes before a fall.

5. Don't overreact.

Panic-driven overreaction compounds instability. The role of the leader in stormy seas is to keep perspective and make pragmatic decisions to keep the ship afloat and balance its load.

6. Stay positive and stay confident.

The crew takes their cues from you as a leader. Ultimately, our confidence must come from the Lord. I am often reminded of this quote from the movie Rudy, "There is a God, and [we are] not Him." God is not wringing his hands with worry about how this is all going to turn out, and neither should we.

> "If any of you lacks wisdom, let him ask God, who gives generously to all without reproach, and it will be given him. But let him ask in faith, with no doubting, for the one who doubts is like a wave of the sea that is driven and tossed by the wind. For that person must not suppose that he will receive anything from the Lord; he is a double-minded man, unstable in all his ways."
>
> *– James 1:1-8*

About The Center Consulting Group

We are 100% focused on leaders.
With Christian values as our organization's foundation, our mission is to help leaders in businesses, nonprofits, and churches lead well.

We make you our first priority.
We have nothing to gain by "selling" you services you do not need.

We customize our services for you.
Our team of experienced consultants and staff customizes services for you and your organization's needs.

We listen and learn to help you lead.
We make sure we fully understand your unique context, vision, and needs before we recommend the services we believe will provide the solutions for your needs.

We build long-lasting relational connections.
We stay connected to many of our clients long after the contract has ended. In fact, many of our clients have contracted with us multiple times over many years.

We not only provide solutions, we help you implement them.
Our consultants work with you and your other leaders by providing ongoing coaching, encouragement, and accountability to increase your success.

Our Solutions

- Leadership Coaching
- Leader & Staffing Assessment
- Team Development
- Crisis Guidance
- Personalized Coaching Retreats
- Staffing Guidance
- Human Resource Guidance
- Strategic Action Planning
- Succession Planning
- Board/Owner Advising
- New Market Assessment and Development
- Merger/Acquisition Guidance and Coaching

Contact Us

The Center Consulting Group is passionate about advancing leadership and organizational health. Whether you are a leader of a values-based business, nonprofit, or church, our experienced team will create customized solutions to help you lead well.

To learn more about how our team can assist you, please contact us at **215-723-2325** or visit our website, **www.centerconsulting.org**.

Assessment Tools

Leader 360° Process

This process includes gathering anonymous perspectives of how your leadership is viewed by you, your supervisor(s), your peers, and those who report to you. Such feedback is one of the most accurate ways to identify strengths, areas of improvement, and possible blind spots.

Personality Testing

Our personality assessments provide a variety of insights into an individual's behaviors, motivators, strengths, areas of development, traditional personality traits, and job-centered behavioral characteristics. They can be used for both pre-hire screening and coaching an employee or team of employees.

Stress Assessment

This stress assessment reveals the stressors at work in your organization. It examines seven different types of stress in individuals and their causes. This can be used in coaching an employee or for a team training.

Group Assessments

Board Assessment: Includes a survey and/or confidential phone interviews of board members to identify strengths, perceptions, and areas of improvement.

Employee Satisfaction Survey: Includes a survey of your employees to identify perceptions regarding job satisfaction, benefits, morale, and other themes.

Organizational Health Assessment

This assessment includes our custom-designed surveys, confidential interviews, and facilitated discussions about your organizational health and the relational health of your team to give you objectivity and foresight in making wise decisions.

Endorsements

"Our organization has recently been going through a rather unique succession process at one of the most difficult times in our history, and we would not have been able to navigate our way through it without The Center's guidance and expertise. All of their staff are wonderful and so generous in the help and kindness they offer. Every person is real, relational, and full of wisdom and experience." –Center Client

"We have used The Center's services to present principles of organizational and behavioral management for our entire team as well as one on one confidential coaching. The broad range of experiences represented by their group provides the opportunity to discuss situations with advisors who have been there." –Center Client

"Our organization recently experienced a significant time of difficulty including interpersonal conflict and organizational disruption among our senior leaders. We are very grateful to The Center for the assistance the consulting team provided with the fact-finding process to help us listen, learn, and make wise (objective) decisions. The entire team is highly credentialed and has extensive experience. Overall, The Center was so good that we hired them to provide ongoing coaching, encouragement, and accountability for our senior leadership. We are in a better place and stronger as a result of working with The Center." –Center Client

"The Center has been very helpful to me personally on several occasions. They are excellent at helping individuals and organizations understand next steps for growth and expansion. I have come to rely on The Center for clear, concise solutions to organizational problems." –Center Client

About the Authors

 Jay Desko is the President and CEO of The Center Consulting Group located in Dublin, Pennsylvania. Jay brings experience in the areas of organizational assessment, leadership coaching, decision-making, and strategic questioning. Jay's degrees include an M.Ed. in Instructional Systems Design and a Ph.D. in Organizational Behavior and Leadership. If you would like to contact Jay, he can be reached at jdesko@centerconsulting.org.

 Dave Marks is a Senior Consultant at The Center Consulting Group located in Dublin, PA. Dave has over 35 years of church ministry experience including 23 years as a senior pastor. His consulting experience includes ministry assessment, leadership coaching, and strategic planning. His degrees include an M.S. in Organizational Leadership and a D.Min in Leadership. If you would like to contact Dave, he can be reached at dmarks@centerconsulting.org.